To Jean
with best wishes,

Ulrich

1-20-2014

MONASTIC PRISONS
AND TORTURE CHAMBERS

Monastic Prisons
and
Torture Chambers

Crime and Punishment in Central
European Monasteries, 1600–1800

ULRICH L. LEHNER

 CASCADE *Books* · Eugene, Oregon

MONASTIC PRISONS AND TORTURE CHAMBERS
Crime and Punishment in Central European Monasteries,
1600–1800

Cascade Books
An Imprint of Wipf and Stock Publishers
199 W. 8th Ave., Suite 3
Eugene, OR 97401

www.wipfandstock.com

ISBN 13: 978-1-62564-040-6

Cataloguing-in-Publication data:

Lehner, Ulrich L., 1976–

  Monastic prisons and torture chambers : crime and punishment in central european monasteries, 1600–1800 / Ulrich L.
Lehner.

  xii + 106 pp. ; 23 cm. Includes bibliographical references.

  ISBN 13: 978-1-62564-040-6

  1. Monasticism and religious orders—History—Modern
period, 1500–. 2. Prisons—History. 3. Crime—Europe, Central—
History. I. Title.

BX2820 .L44 2013

Manufactured in the U.S.A.

Alphonso Huber—
magistro quondam meo dilectissimo

Contents

Preface | ix

Introduction: Legends, Myths, and
Misconceptions | 1

1 Confinement for Criminals and the Insane—
Differences between Orders and Genders | 11

2 What Was a Monastic Prison Like? | 17

3 Orders with and without "Prisons": Differences
between Orders and Genders | 32

4 The Franciscan "Criminal Trial" | 38

5 Physical Assault and Assassination Attempts in
Female Convents | 67

6 Fornication and Child Abuse | 73

7 Escapes from the Cloister | 81

Conclusion | 89

Bibliography | 91

Preface

So this is the castle of your ideas—now show me the dungeon.

ROBERT GRAY[1]

THIS BOOK WAS NEVER intended, and the fact that it was written is due to a number of circumstances I should like to explain. When I began research for a new book on monasticism and the Enlightenment in 2008,[2] I stumbled upon the writings of former monks denouncing inhumane treatment within the cloister and describing gruesome monastic prisons. Since I had never heard of monastic prisons before, I attempted to find out more about these institutions, without much success. Moreover, the literature I found was either apologetic or anticlerical—a fact that bothered me deeply. Consequently, I started searching through archival material for files that might contain material about monastic criminal trials and prisons, with the intention of publishing a small article about it. Once I began consulting the rules of

1. Gray, *Lineations*, 106. I thank my friend Kevin Hart (University of Virginia) for bringing this epigram to my attention.

2. Lehner, *Enlightened Monks*.

the different religious orders in order to see how each group treated its prisoners, I realized that the topic warranted a little book. As such, it is by no means an exhaustive history of crime and punishment in early modern monasticism, but rather a guide to completely overlooked fields of research—such as criminal law in monastic settings, church and state conflicts regarding criminal lawsuits, violence in monasteries, monastic gender research and monastic mentality, the development of criminal law and criminal investigation, and so forth.

Reconstructing a culture of crime and punishment, of torture and inhumane treatment, was a personal challenge and an unpleasant experience. Nevertheless, as a historian I am convinced that such a reconstruction is necessary for a better understanding of early modern Catholicism, and consequently also early modern culture; and as a theologian I believe that "only the truth will set [us] free" (John 8:32). Although the following pages might prove embarrassing for a Catholic to read, a thorough analysis of crime in Catholic religious communities should not overshadow the great efforts of the early modern orders in helping the poor, lonely, and marginalized, or their striving for a holy life and a reform of the church.[3]

My colleagues in the Marquette Theology Department encouraged me to pursue the quest for historical truth in moments when I wanted to give it up. I thank in particular Ralph del Colle (†), D. Stephen Long, Daniel C. Maguire, and Mickey Mattox for their friendship and reassurance. Furthermore, Chad Pecknold, School of Theology and Religious Studies of the Catholic University of America; Julius Ruff, Marquette University History Department; and Daniel-Odon Hurel, Universitè Jean Monnet/Saint-Étienne,

3. See, for example, Châtellier, *The Religion of the Poor*; Châtellier, *The Europe of the Devout*; Bedouelle, *The Reform of Catholicism*.

provided assistance and helpful feedback. I am also indebted to many archives, especially those of the Haus-, Hof- und Staatsarchiv of Vienna and the Diocesan Archive of Trier. While some religious orders were extremely helpful (in particular, the Capuchins in Altötting), others insisted that no files existed about eighteenth-century disciplinary cases or that their orders never had "monastic prisons"—even if their own constitutions proved otherwise.

One order in particular will be associated with monastic prisons after reading this book—the Capuchins. I would like to state for the record that I have nothing against this order but only followed the evidence I found in archival and printed sources. In fact, two of my uncles were Capuchins, and while I doubt they would have found this book enjoyable reading, I think they would have wanted it to be published.

I would like to dedicate this book first and foremost to my first teacher of history, Alphons Huber, a role model of academic precision and congeniality, who inspired my interest in paleography and archival studies at the tender age of twelve. Second, I wish to dedicate it to my relatives and friends in religious orders, who have shown me the beauty and candor of a religious vocation.

Milwaukee, Wisconsin
19 March 2013

Introduction

Legends, Myths, and Misconceptions

WHEREVER PEOPLE STRIVE FOR holiness, there is also sin, as the road to perfection is a long and difficult journey on which not everyone will prevail. It should therefore not surprise us that sinful behavior occurs also in monasteries. Yet, why should historians and scholars of religion care about how monasteries dealt with severe sins or even crimes within their communities?

There are a number of answers to such a legitimate question. First, monastic rules about criminal trials and imprisonment demonstrate the convoluted relationship between canon law and the development of modern judicial practices. Today we take the right to a defense counsel for granted, without realizing that such a practice made its way into modern law through the rules of inquisitorial trials conducted under canon law.[1] Likewise, the history of monastic prisons sheds new light on the use of torture within monastic communities, and as such provides a better understanding of violence among persons who considered themselves "family." Second, a history of monastic prisons

---

1. Trusen, "Inquisitionsprozess."

1

and trials demonstrates that church leaders were eager to avoid public scandal, even if it meant lying to state authorities or disobeying their laws. This medieval pattern continued throughout the early modern period and was not eradicated until the beginning of the twenty-first century. Third, since monasteries were an essential part of European and transatlantic Catholic culture, investigating the culture of law, crime, and punishment in these communities helps us to gain a better understanding of monasticism after the Council of Trent (1545–1563)—in particular, how religious orders attempted to create a sacred space within the cloister from which they separated convicted criminals. Paying attention to crimes within the cloister also enriches the picture we have of such communities. Such a glimpse into the "dark" sides of monasticism is necessary for a vivid and convincing narrative about the "inner life" of early modern Catholic monasticism.[2] Fourth, especially during the eighteenth century, the judicial sovereignty of monasteries was questioned or denied by state authorities. Therefore, monastic criminal trials became during this time a hotbed of state-church conflicts, and our knowledge of these trials contributes to a better understanding of the relationship of church and state during the "long" eighteenth century. Fifth, monastic criminal law enables historians to reconstruct a forgotten gender perspective and to determine differences between female and male religious in regard to crime and punishment. Last but not least, a treatment of monastic prisons seems necessary due to widespread legends and rumors about them, in particular in anti-Catholic writings. A thorough historical account may help one discern what is legend, myth, misconception, or historical truth.

Another question is why, among historians, monastic prisons remain largely unknown. Despite the fact that

2. For this approach, see Rothschild, *Inner Life of Empires.*

even the Carmelite saint and mystic John of the Cross (1542–1591) suffered in a monastic dungeon for an entire year (1577–78),[3] the post-Reformation monastery "prison" (*carcer, ergastulum*) as a facility of confinement and correction[4] for religious[5] has vanished from historical awareness. Even standard works on the history of Catholicism and on prisons and punishment mention monasteries only in passing and avoid the question of what they did with their "criminals," or those who had committed offenses against the regulations of the order, canon law, or the moral teachings of the Bible. This is even more surprising if one considers that in the case of grave offenses, a "criminal trial" was conducted according to the regulations of canon law and of the particular order.[6]

It is the goal of this book to demonstrate that monastic prisons and trial procedures were a complex part

3. Egan, "John of the Cross," 282–83.

4. Cf. the contemporary definition of prison in Garner, *Black's Law Dictionary*, 1213.

5. The term *religious* is in a Catholic context not just an adjective but also a noun signifying members of religious orders.

6. Not even the excellent overview of early modern attitudes to crime and punishment by van Dülmen, *Theater des Schreckens*, mentions monastic prisons. Evans, *Fabrication of Virtue*, 57–59, merely mentions Mabillon's reflections on the reform of monastic imprisonment in passing. The notable exception for a general work is Chadwick, *Popes and European Revolution*, 239–44. For the most exhaustive analyses of early modern monastic life, including some material on monastic prisons, see the magisterial works of Beales, *Prosperity and Plunder*, and Rapley, *Social History of the Cloister*. A few others include Ammerer, *Orte der Verwahrung*, and Lesaulnier, *Port-Royal et la prison*. Russian literature on monastery prisons focuses mainly on monasteries as prisons for laypeople rather than members of the order; see Shubin, *Monastery Prisons*. An overview of the files on monastery prisons for monks and nuns in the Habsburg territories is offered by Mikoletzky, "Klosterkerker–Korrektionshäuser." On the situation in Savoy, see Meyer, "Religiosi fuorillege."

of cloistered life that shaped the dynamics of monasticism between the Reformation and the Enlightenment, and to introduce the reader to a number of fields of research. The focus is on central Europe, although comparisons with other European states are also mentioned. Moreover, it will become clear that examining the history of these prisons can be useful in gaining fresh insights into the history of sacred and profane space. When monks and nuns were imprisoned, religious authorities regarded them as if they were no longer part of the sacred space of their community. Nevertheless, these people could be asked to accept their fate as an earthly purgatory and thus their last chance for redemption. The history of monastic prisons shows that within this context, there was not much difference between being punished for a sin, a crime, or breaking ecclesiastical law. The distinction between them was less important than protecting and maintaining a flawless, sacred monastic space, which was supported by the existence of such prisons. Unlike their urban medieval counterparts, the monastic prison was mostly exclusive to the particular monastery and inaccessible to the outside world. While small misdemeanors did not yet signal the severing of ties to the rest of the community, an escape attempt from the cloister could.

Based on archival and printed sources, I will attempt to give an account of what life in monastic prisons was like, who was subjected to confinement, and under what conditions. Moreover, I will also demonstrate that confinement in a monastery coexisted, as in secular institutions of the period, with corporal punishment and did not replace it. While I refer to a number of printed sources from all over Europe, the archival evidence is primarily from the Holy Roman Empire.

Monastic prisons, which were not freestanding houses of correction but usually basement cells or specially designated rooms within the monastery, are not mentioned by Michel Foucault (1926–1984) in his *Surveiller et punir* (1975), who argued that prisons did not become accepted penal institutions until around 1800 and claimed that early modern incarceration cells were predominantly for beggars, vagrants, or debtors. Pieter Spierenburg's groundbreaking book *The Prison Experience* (1991), which refuted many of Foucault's central claims,[7] also does not mention monastic prisons, although his argument that secular prisons were established specifically for criminals in the Netherlands and Germany (and no longer for vagrants) by the second half of the seventeenth century could have been strengthened by reference to monastic prisons.[8]

Although there is an abundance of data on this issue, why have scholars so consistently neglected it?[9] One reason was that some historians were overcautious and considered anti-monastic literature[10] and pseudo-scientific treatments[11] of the subject, which portrayed religious

7. Foucault, *Überwachen und Strafen*, 295–329. In *The Prison Experience: Disciplinary Institutions in Early Modern Europe*, Spierenburg refutes a number of Foucault's claims—for example, that the prison system came into existence around 1800. Instead, he shows that a fully working prison system existed in Hamburg/Germany and the Netherlands from the end of the seventeenth century. On the incarceration of debtors in medieval times, see Geltner, *Medieval Prison*, 46–47.

8. Spierenburg, *Prison Experience*, 135–70.

9. See, for example, Cassidy-Welch, *Imprisonment in the Medieval Religious Imagination*.

10. For the vast anti-monastic German literature, see Jäger, "Mönchskritik und Klostersatire in der deutschen Spätaufklärung"; for Italian accounts, see the discussion of forced monachitation of women and their fate in Schutte, *By Force and Fear*, 23–51.

11. The best example is Ignaz von Born's *Monachology or Natural History of the Monks according to the Linnaean System*, published initially under the pseudonym Kutschenpeitscher, *Neueste Naturgeschichte des Mönchthums* (1802), later published under the title *Monachologie*. Another example is Weber, *Möncherey*.

houses as places of tyranny and violence, as pure fantasy. Another is that historiographical research on early modern and modern monasteries was until recently left almost entirely to ecclesiastical historians, which further contributed to the problem because they often whitewashed the history of the Catholic Church.[12] The idea that religious personally tortured other religious was an intolerable thought that had to be eradicated from institutional memory.[13] Moreover, historians might have dismissed the subject of monastic prisons because sources are extremely hard to find. Often one has to dig through hundreds of pages of visitation protocols in order to finally obtain a few scraps of information about the community prison. Many times, material is hidden in the annals of an order's province or in otherwise inconspicuous files about disciplinary problems.[14] One also finds information about

12. A striking example of deliberate whitewashing is Wiedemann, "Klosterkerker in der Erzdiözese Wien." Likewise, eighteenth-century accounts of monastic prisons, especially from the time of their destruction in the last quarter of the eighteenth century, were considered repetitions of medieval tales, because the existence of monastic and ecclesiastical prisons in the Middle Ages is adequately established (see Cassidy-Welch, *Imprisonment in the Medieval Religious Imagination*). One of the few exceptions is the detailed study by Hurel, "La prison et la charité." The six volumes of Holsten and Brockie, *Codex Regularum Monasticarum et Canonicarum*, remain an indispensable tool for researching the constitutions of ancient and early modern orders.

13. See, for example, Held, *Jurisprudentia universalis*, ch. 4, num. lvii, 254: "clericos et regulares torqueri posse . . ."

14. A good example of this is the file about a Carthusian who left the cloister at night to break the strict vegetarian fasting with pork sausages, because such a person was punished with incarceration— see Bischöfliches Zentralarchiv Regensburg: Kartause Prüll, KL 31a Nr. 8, fol. 4v. The Carthusian Johann Nepomuk Mayr escaped on Christmas Eve 1789 after having periodically left the cloister in secret for several weeks or months. Allegedly, besides his love for sausages, he also began a relationship with a girl.

these prisons in the constitutions of the orders, which despite their importance remain mostly unread by historians. Details about monastic prisons are also described in the autobiographies of former monks. Only records of official criminal trials against monks and nuns are extremely rare.[15]

This, however, is not surprising and should not be considered proof for the nonexistence of such prisons. The reason for the scarcity of this sort of documentation is more than just polite "discretion."[16] Criminal monks (and nuns) were an embarrassment, and it was the duty of every religious community to preserve the good reputation of the order (*fama ordinis*) and to avoid scandal.[17] As a consequence, sensitive documents were destroyed so that they could never fall into the wrong hands. The Carthusian statutes of 1582, for example, prescribe the destruction of visitation protocols every two years in order to ensure that nobody could ever gain information about disciplinary problems in the order.[18] In their 1782 constitutions, the Piarists required that anyone who betrayed the secrets of the order (*extraneis sive secularibus*)

15. The criminal records in this book are mostly only in existence because of some involvement of a local bishop. A rare exception of a trial record that can be found within a monastic archive is that of Bernhard Weinberger of Benediktbeuern (1753); see Hauptstaatsarchiv München: Bayerische Benediktinerkongregation, Rubrik 48 Benediktbeuern, Nr. 6.

16. Hurel, "La prison," 122.

17. On the avoidance of scandal as a legal category, see Fossier, "Propter vitandum scandalum."

18. *Annales Ordinis Cartusiensis,* vol. 1, ch. 8, sect. 3 ("de capitulo de reprehensione"), num. 32–34. See also Rüthing, "Wächter Israels. Ein Beitrag zur Geschichte der Visitationen im Kartäuserorden," 174, 176, 182. For the Franciscans, see *Codex Redactus Legum Fratrum Minorum,* ch. XXXVII–*Capitulum General Paduae (1443),* num. 57, 66: "Secreta nostra non revelentur alicui extra ordinem."

and dishonored (*infamia*) the community had to spend at least six months in prison.[19] The Franciscans had a similar rule.[20] Only the Hieronymites of Spain explicitly mention that the protocols of criminal trials should be kept in the central archive of the province.[21]

Such "discretion" for the sake of the order's reputation seems to have condoned deceiving the secular authorities.

---

19. *Constitutiones Religionis Clericorum Regularium Pauperum Matris Dei Scholarum Piarum*, Canones Poenitentales, cap. 11 (De poena Revelantium Secreta Congregationis), 347. See also the constitutions of the Hieronymites, *Constitutiones et Extravagantes Ordinis monachorum St. Hieronymi*, pars. 29, 70, which explicitly proscribe revealing what punishments religious have to suffer: "Caveant monachi . . . vel indirecte verbo, aut scripto, per se, aut per alios, quomodo-libet manifestare, aut revelare praesumant culpas graves, poenasque propter eas ipsis impositis: unde gravis infamia, & manifestum dede-cus nostro Ordini subsequi, & imminere possit." The Augustinian Canons had a similar rule, which Eusebius Amort reported in his *Vetus Disciplina Canonicorum Regularium et Saecularium*, vol. 2, pt. 2, cap. 13, 878. It lists specific disciplinary problems and deficiencies of the personnel that should never be revealed to the laity. See also the rules of the Camillian order, *Regula et Constitutiones Clericorum Regularium Ministrantium Infirmis*, 93: "Si quis secreta nostrae religionis explicaverit. Per secreta religionis intelliguntur omnia, ob quorum revelationem religioni provincia, monasterio, aut particulari personae grave prejudicium vel detrimentum evenire possit." The Servites in Germany punished a revealer of secrets with three years (!) in prison and deprivation of voting rights for five years; see Gün-therode, *Römische Religionskasse*, 3:283.

20. Since according to Franciscan regulations perpetual impris-onment could only be inflicted with knowledge of the provincial council, the following statute of the General Chapter of 1694 can also be applied to divulging knowledge about imprisoned monks: "Ne-mini, sub poenis gravissimis, liceat revelare ea, quae discussa sunt in consultatione, culpiam extra ipsam" (*Codex Redactus Legum Fratrum Minorum*, ch. LXXVIII—*Capitulum Generale Victoriae (1694)*, num. 25, 418). See also *Constitutiones Urbanae Ordinis*, 303, can. 7.

21. *Constitutiones et Extravagantes Ordinis Monachorum S. Hi-eronymi*, 44.

When Habsburg Emperor Joseph II (r. 1780–1790) sent an official commission to Capuchin monasteries to inquire about the existence of forbidden dungeons in 1783, the Capuchins lied to government officials about their archival documentation of judicial cases.[22] The Augustinian abbot of Klosterneuburg, outside Vienna, also wrongfully claimed that his house did not have a monastic prison,[23] and the Dominican prioress of Kirchberg feigned surprise when state officials found an (empty) dungeon in her monastery.[24] Not only did religious orders misinform secular authorities, but they also pretended to be ignorant of legislation that outlawed monastic prisons. An old dungeon was cheaper than keeping an insane religious in an asylum, and more secure if the religious was a criminal convicted by canon law and monastic rules. Maria Theresa (r. 1740–1780) abolished the prisons in 1771 for the Habsburg lands, but in 1783 the prior of the Capuchins in Braunau claimed he was not aware of such laws because his monastery had belonged to Bavaria until 1779. In the library there, state commissioners found a copy of the law that had been mailed the year before to all monasteries, which proved that the prior had lied.[25] In the Galician Augustinian monastery of Zalozce, the prior ignored the

22. Allgemeines Verwaltungsarchiv Wien: Bestand Alter Kultus, kath. Kirche 619, Sign. 63, Generalia, 339 ex 1783, Report of the Commission, signed by Hägele, to Count Pergen, undated, 109.

23. Wiedemann, "Klosterkerker," 431.

24. Hauptstaatsarchiv Stuttgart: B 40 Bü 478 (on the abolition of monastic prisons in the county of Rottenburg).

25. *Allgemeines Verwaltungsarchiv Wien:* Bestand Alter Kultus, kath. Kirche 619, Sign. 63, Generalia, 179 ex 1783, Report of the Local Commission in Linz to the Geistliche Hofkommission of 23 April 1783; Geistliche Hofkommission to Joseph II 13 May 1783, fol. 11–12. For his inhumane treatment of Fr. Loginus the prior was deposed and punished.

new law and imprisoned monks as late as 1781, put them on the rack, or hit them with a stick up to three hundred times a day.[26] In addition to religious orders, bishops also viewed this legislation as an infringement upon their traditional jurisdiction. Even the archbishop of Vienna, Cardinal Migazzi (1714–1803), was unofficially accused of concealing the existence of monastic prisons.[27] Only the severe punishment of such superiors by state authorities and the threat of closing monasteries that did not comply with the law helped improve the situation in the Habsburg lands.

Finally, monastic prisons might have been neglected by historians because they were considered to be like early modern prisons, serving only semi-penal or even non-penal purposes such as separating a monk from his community or disciplining him.[28] Monastic confinement was then of course no longer taken seriously as punishment for a "crime," but seen as a precursor to modern methods of discipline and compared to the chastisement of nineteenth-century factory workers[29] or the secular prison as a "spatial solution for public order problems."[30]

26. Allgemeines Verwaltungsarchiv Wien: Alter Kultus, Kath. Kirche, sign. 63, Galizien, 74 ex Februario 1784, fol. 1316.

27. Allgemeines Verwaltungsarchiv Wien: Bestand Alter Kultus, kath. Kirche 619, Sign. 63, Generalia, 339 ex 1783, Report of the Commission, signed by Hägele, to Count Pergen, undated, 111–17.

28. Cf. Spierenburg, *Prison Experience*, 5.

29. Treiber and Steinert, *Fabrikation des zuverlässigen Menschen*.

30. Spierenburg, "From Amsterdam to Auburn," 441.

1

Confinement for Criminals and the Insane

Differences between Orders and Genders

A MONASTIC PRISON HAD three purposes. It was a penitentiary for those who could be reintegrated into the community, an ordinary prison for incorrigible religious who had proved to be irreformable, and a space of confinement for the mentally disturbed.[1]

While it was common knowledge that monasteries dealt with mentally unstable people in this way, ecclesiastical

1. The following paragraph is based on the overview in Lehner, *Enlightened Monks*, 103–5. See also Kober, "Gefängnisstrafe gegen Cleriker und Mönche"; Kober, "Körperliche Züchtigung als kirchliches Strafmittel gegen Kleriker und Mönche." For Benedictines see also Spilker, "Busspraxis in der Regel des hl. Benedikt"; Heufelder, "Strenge und Milde: Die Strafkapitel der Benediktinerregel"; Hofmeister, "Vom Strafverfahren bei den Ordensleuten." For the history of ecclesiastical prisons in general, see Krauss, *Im Kerker vor und nach Christus.*

historians often claimed that the fate of such monks and nuns was no worse than in the secular world. While this is true for severe cases, it is not so for milder ones. A mildly disturbed layperson could still live in freedom and was not confined to a dungeon, but until the end of the eighteenth century, religious who were likewise disturbed—even if nonviolent—were kept in the monastery prison, and like the mentally unstable in the secular world, "treated" with corporal punishment.[2] The Austrian Capuchin brother Nemesian Peikl (d. 1784) was imprisoned in 1728 and not transferred to a psychiatric hospital until 1783. His was probably not a severe case of insanity; in fact, some sources describe him as weird but mentally lucid.[3] His behavior, however, was embarrassing: "He kneels in front of others, walks into the garden, serves others and helps them carry water."[4] According to the general statutes of the order, genuflecting in front of others was an offense that carried a prison sentence, a fact that the monks did not find necessary to

2. The case of Benedict Bräutigam of the Charterhouse Mainz, who had been imprisoned in a miserable dungeon for ten years until detected by state officials in 1773, can be found in Mangei, "Klosterhaft und Klosterregel–Aussenseiter in monastischen Gemeinschaften," 61; Simmert, *Geschichte der Kartause zu Mainz*, 63–64. On secular hospitals and the care for mentally ill, see Vanja, "Madhouses, Children's Wards, and Clinics"; see also the important collection by Grell et al., *Health Care and Poor Relief in 18th and 19th Century Southern Europe*. The classical treatments are Foucault, *Madness and Civilization*, and Porter, *Madness*.

3. Scherhak, "Klosterkerker," 100. Despite the fact that he had an early episode of violence, this seems to have been a singular event. He is consistently described as peaceful and a "holy lunatic."

4. Allgemeines Verwaltungsarchiv Wien: Bestand Alter Kultus, kath. Kirche 619, Sign. 63, Generalia, 339 ex 1783, Summarische Aussage of 19 February 1783, fol. 86. The monastery pharmacist Br. Dionysios confirms that Nemesian "genuflects" in front of everybody (fol. 91), but also that he regularly confesses and receives communion.

reveal to visiting government officials.[5] Yet another example
is that of the Capuchin Fr. Thuribius. In Poysdorf, Austria,
he was confined to prison for being restless, shouting, and
not keeping his unheated room clean. He was beaten by his
own confreres often at their own will, and "whenever the
prior got in a rage . . . he had [P. Thuribius] dragged into
the library, where he would flog him with ox strings until
he was unable to move."[6] The prior, deposed by Joseph II
for his inhumane behavior, defended his actions in 1783 by
stating that Thuribius was either insane and required such
treatment because of his disease, or a bad person in need of
punishment. It is also questionable whether the treatment
of insane laypeople in monasteries was preferable to that
in a secular institution (as is sometimes claimed by church
historians), as a report about the treatment of inmates in
the monastery of the Alexian brothers in Neuss near Cologne of 1781 shows. The patients and prison inmates were
deprived not only of proper clothes but also of decent food
and physical exercise, and they had to endure the violence
of the brothers, who often employed it to "treat" their
patients.[7]

5. *Statuta Generalia Cismontanae Familiae Ordinis Fratrum Minorum Sancti Francisci Reformatorum in capitulo generali Anno 1639*
(Prague: 1677), ch. 7 (Applicatio singularum poenarum singulis delictis), num. 6: ". . . genuflexus in publico . . . debet in pane & aqua
jejunare, ac omni suffragiorum jure biennio carcere."

6. Allgemeines Verwaltungsarchiv Wien: Bestand Alter Kultus,
kath. Kirche 619, Sign. 63, Generalia, 339 ex 1783, Relation und
Kommissions Protokoll of 4 February 1783, fol. 68–69. Although
forbidden, priors seem to frequently have used unheated cells to punish their religious, often with the consequence of severe frostbite. See
Anonymous, "Gesinnungen eines österreichischen Mönches nach
der Aufhebung seines Klosters," 275.

7. Staatsarchiv Düsseldorf: Kurköln VIIIm 795: Letter of Carl
Nesselrod to the Archbishop Elector of Cologne of 7 December 1781.

Monastic Prisons and Torture Chambers

The use of monastic cells as penitentiary rooms increased during the late Middle Ages. While in earlier periods of church history monks and nuns could be expelled for apostasy, attempted marriage, heresy or schism, blasphemy, violence against clergymen, theft, abortion, participation in a duel, homicide, abduction of minors, sexual relations with a minor under the age of sixteen, homosexuality and bestiality, etc., such expulsions were rare after the thirteenth century due to papal law. By the 1500s, expulsions from centralist orders were reserved to the generals of the orders in Rome.[8] Perpetual imprisonment in a monastic dungeon became the usual sentence for crimes that would have been punished by death under secular law.[9] Thus, a monastery prison indeed replaced the death penalty, but this did not mean that such a verdict excluded additional corporal punishment, as the history of the secular prison would suggest. Instead, even monks who had been sentenced to life in prison often had to undergo harmful physical punishment.[10] Pope Pius IV (1559–1565) confirmed the usefulness of monastic prisons, and only a few orders, like the Jesuits, received the papal privilege of expelling incorrigible members.[11] Less egregious

8. O'Leary, *Religious Dismissed after Perpetual Profession*, 53–54; Hofmeister, "Vom Strafverfahren," 33. Cf. Hartmann, *Kirche und Kirchenrecht um 900*; Kéry, *Gottesfurcht und irdische Strafe*.

9. Kober, "Gefängnissstrafe gegen Cleriker und Mönche," 558, 562. It is important to remember that the *Code of Law of Maria Theresa* (1766) demanded the death penalty for murder, blasphemy, sorcery, apostasy, sacrilege, infanticide, and attempted suicide (Beales, *Joseph II,* 548–50).

10. On the question whether the modern prison functioned as an alternative to physical punishment, see Spierenburg, "Four Centuries of Prison History."

11. O'Leary, *Religious Dismissed,* 11–22; cf. Logan, *Runaway,* 4–8. On the restrictions of expulsions from religious orders, see Scherhak, "Klosterkerker," 25–30; Kober, "Gefängnisstrafe," 69; Heufelder, "Strenge." For Urban VIII's decree *Sacra Congregatio* of

crimes were punished with proportionate amounts of time in prison, but each order and sometimes each province had its own peculiarities. The Recollect Franciscans of Flanders stated in their statutes of 1718 that each convent had to have at least two cells that could be used for incarcerating a friar.[12] The Spanish Hieronymites punished those monks who permitted or attended profane theater plays with six months' suspension from office.[13] Theft and excessive gambling also were punished severely.[14]

Leaving the monastery illicitly, that is, trying to escape, was grounds for being treated as an apostate. However, Pope Urban VIII (1623–1644) instituted a more lenient rule, stating that if one returned within four months to his home monastery without having committed other crimes (apostasy, adultery, fornication, etc.), one could be reconciled with the monastic community without serious repercussions. However, this rule was limited to the cisalpine religious.[15] It is indeed remarkable that a considerable number of runaway religious eventually returned to their monasteries in such a manner.[16] Common motives for escape were problems with the community—such as

---

1694, which further restricted expulsions, see Hofmeister, "Vom Strafverfahren," 34–35.

12. *Statuta Provincilia,* 46.

13. *Constitutiones et Extravagantes Ordinis Monachorum S. Hieronymi,* 71. Also, no one could be received into the order who descended in the fourth degree from Jews or Muslims (83–84). Similar admonitions about theater plays, but also visits to inns and breweries, are given in the circulars of the Thuringian Franciscans. See Plath, "Beispiel klösterlichers Jurisdiktion im 18. Jahrhundert," 272.

14. *Regula et Constitutiones Clericorum regularium ministrantium infirmis* (1727), 92.

15. Riesner, *Apostates and Fugitives from Religious Institutes,* 34, 39, 44–46.

16. Cf. Logan, *Runaway Religious,* 121–55.

discontentment with spiritual progress, boredom, personal desire for material possessions or sexual relations, and problems with the vow of obedience. Escaping, however, was generally something resorted to after all legitimate alternatives, like being transferred to a different monastery, had been exhausted.[17] Sometimes very mundane reasons like bad food or drink could motivate a religious to escape. In 1788 the Benedictine Ludolph Stollreither ran away from his abbey Schäftlarn in Bavaria because he could not digest the heavy beer in the monastery. He returned after a few weeks (and was not punished) when the abbot promised him good light wheat beer instead.[18]

17. Logan, *Runaway Religious,* 42–65. The Norbertines had a special statute that mentioned the case of a *"lapsus carnis"* with female members of the order, for example, impregnating them (*impraegnaverint vel cognoverint*), which was harshly punished; see Holsten and Brockie, *Codex Regularum,* 5:283.

18. Bayerisches Hauptstaatsarchiv München: Kurbaiern Geistlicher Rat, Aufsicht über die Klöster, vorl. Sign. Schaeftlarn 24, Letter of the Abbot of 18 July 1788 to the Bavarian Elector, and Letter of L. Stollreither of 24 July 1788 to the Elector.

2

What Was a Monastic Prison Like?

THE MILDEST PUNISHMENT FOR a religious was the official admonition of the superior. If this did not work, smaller punishments for coming too late to prayer or other such trivial offences might include sitting on the floor during common meals or taking the last, most junior spot in choir. Only if the preservation of discipline required more severe steps were monks or nuns excluded from the community, and then either confined to an honorable or dishonorable prison, which sometimes consisted of separate rooms or a common room. The honorable prison was often a regular cell that could be locked, and religious were usually not deprived of pious books, voting rights, and regular food, despite routine, compulsory fasting.[1] Its severity could be increased, but as such it was a punishment that only

1. For severe crimes, extreme fasting (bread and water) could be increased to three days a week; this sanction was, however, almost never executed in a secular prison. Spierenburg, *Prison Experience*, 16.

separated the errant religious from the rest of the community for a while in order to make him rethink his ways.

The dishonorable prison (*carcer, ergastulum*) was a
holding cell for criminal religious, and often only a subter-
ranean dungeon. Inmates lost the right to vote in monastery
elections, as well as most of their other rights. The Council
of Trent (1545–1563) never abolished the *poena carceris*
and it remained a regular means of improving the moral
status of the clergy in the post-Tridentine Church, whether
in a diocese or a monastery, until the nineteenth century.[2]

Augustin Calmet (1672–1757), the erudite Benedictine of St. Vanne, explained in his commentary on the rule
of St. Benedict the necessity of a prison and the value of
maintaining discipline within a monastery. While lesser
crimes were punished with separation from the common
table, greater crimes were punished with separation from
the body of the faithful through *excommunication*. This
meant that the delinquent was shunned and separated from
communal prayer. Sometimes the separation from prayer
and common table were combined, and the abbot could
intensify the punishment by adding prison and fasting.[3]

2. For the right of the bishop over his priests, see Concilium
Tridentinum sess. vi, c. 4 de ref.; sess. 14 c. 4 de ref. For his right
to imprison priests, see Concilium Tridentinum sess. xxv, c. 6 and
c. 14. Cf. Kober, "Gefängnisstrafe," 575–76. In fact, the concordat of
1855 between the Papal State and Austria still confirmed the right
of bishops to detain clergymen in seminaries or monasteries (ibid.,
587–88). On diocesan correction facilities, see May, *Priesterhaus;*
Struber, *Priesterkorrektionsanstalten.*

3. Calmet, *Commentarius litteralis,* i: ch. 24, 258: "Opponuntur
culpae illae istis, quae ex malitia, ex prava cordis affectione, inobedi-
entia, superbia, contemptu Regularum, Superioribus illata injuria,
contumacia, incorrigibilitate, aut obduratione fiunt . . . Primi generis
culpae puniuntur per separationem a mensa: aliae vero per separationem a corpore fidelium per excommunicationem majorem." While an
ecclesiastical excommunication (*major ban*) could only be inflicted

Among the offenses that deserved the highest punishment were breaking the vows of obedience, chastity, and poverty, but also frequent and scandalous relations with women, rage, violence, theft, and all other mortal sins that caused scandal inside or outside the community and therefore disturbed the peace (*pax conventus perturbari*). For severe offenses, Calmet wrote, since their beginning in the sixth century the Benedictines have had a prison in which a monk could also be shackled.[4] The statutes of the French Coelestines of 1670 likewise affirmed incarceration for offenses against their constitutions, as well as restraints for hands and feet.[5] In most orders no prior or abbot could send someone to a prison without a formal trial, in which the prior or abbot and usually some senior members of the community were judges.[6] Corporal punishment with rods or straps was common and usually applied to the naked

---

for major crimes, a monastic excommunication could be inflicted on a monk for habitually coming too late to prayer, for eating privately, for laughing in the choir, or for accidentally breaking a vessel. Moreover, while the ecclesiastical excommunication was a *poena medicinalis*, which intended the improvement of the delinquent and could be lifted *only* through a formal act, the monastic equivalent could be inflicted for a certain time and was afterwards automatically lifted, which shows that it was a merely disciplinary action, although most commentators on the rule of St. Benedict understood it to be a major ban (Kober, "Körperliche Züchtigung," 368). The Franciscans did not understand the excommunication in their monasteries as major ban; see, for example, *Regula et Constitutiones Fratrum Poenitentium*, sect. VIII, art. 2, num. 4, 150: "Excommunicationis nomine non intelligimus censuram ecclesiasticam, sed poenam mere regularem."

4. Calmet, *Commentarius litteralis*, ch. 25, 260–61.

5. *Constitutiones Fratrum Coelestinorum Proviniciae Franco-Gallicanae*, lib. III, II pars, 233: ". . . deinde mittatur in carcerem, ubi ferreis vel ligneis (si expediens fuerit) compedibus astringatur . . ."

6. See, for example, the statutes of the Cassinese Benedictine Congregation of 1670 in Güntherode, *Römische Religionskasse,* ii: num. 17, 348.

upper body (back), but it was a punishment inflicted by others almost exclusively in the old pre-Tridentine orders, such as the Trinitarians. Most regulations limited such punishment to the length of the (penitential) Psalm 51 (*Miserere*).[7] The Spanish Trinitarians, for example, had the practice confirmed in 1676 that if a friar committed a crime among secular people, he was to be flagellated by the community and imprisoned for one year.[8] The Spanish Hieronymites, whose constitutions were confirmed in 1730, explained that the sinner had to take off his tunic and be flagellated by the prior in front of the whole convent for grave public sins.[9]

A monastic or any other ecclesiastic dishonorable prison probably did not look much different than a secular dungeon in medieval times, namely "inhuman, frightening and dark . . . humid, cold, and often crawling with snakes and toads," as Felix Fabri described it in 1484.[10] Due to such

7. Kober, "Körperliche Züchtigung," 386. Alternatively, the number of lashes could be determined. Only the *Regula Magistri ad monachos* (6th c.) allows, according to Kober, flagellation "usque ad necem" (until death; ibid., 388). For the Franciscan criminal law, see Sinistrari, *Practica criminalis illustrata*, i: tit. XVI, § 2, 583: "In gravioribus delictis arctatione, flagellis, jejuniis, taxillis, vel sibilis iudices uti permittuntur. Itaut de mendacio, vel de crimine, suspecti nudi, cum solis femoralibus manibus ligati, per tria intervalla flagellis superioris arbitrio dire torqueri possint; et pane et aqua macerari; idque bis vel ter replicari, prout ratio suaserit. Arctatus nesciat tempus, in quo ter in hebdomada in pane & aqua jejunare debet, et sibi disciplinae flagella in publico Refectorio infligere unius *Miserere mei* & c. spatio."

8. At Güntherode, *Römische Religionskasse*, i: num. 17, 196: "Quod si delictum publicum fuerit apud seculares, disciplina conventuali flagelletur . . ." See also *Magnum Bullarium Romanum*, xi: 152.

9. Güntherode, *Römische Religionskasse*, iii: 338–39; see also *Constitutiones et Extravagantes Ordinis Monachorum S. Hieronym*), 68.

10. Geltner, *Medieval Prison*, 72. On medieval monastic prisons, see also Lusset, "Entree le murs"; Pugh, *Imprisonment*; Leclerq, *Libérez*; Cassidy-Welch, "Incarceration."

conditions, canonists regularly admonished religious superiors to be more humane (*humanus*) to their prisoners.[11] The statutes of the Spanish Trinitarians of 1738, published in 1787, still insisted that all monasteries should have a secure prison; however, one "not too rigorous" (*non tamen adeo rigorosus*). It should contain chains for hands and feet (*compedes et vincula*) and all necessary instruments for torture or extra harsh confinement. Nevertheless, the superior was admonished to provide spiritual consolation for the imprisoned. Spiritual books could be read, but writing was proscribed.[12] The Spanish Discalced Carmelites insisted on having prisons in their houses in 1787 and made it clear that they should be secure but not inhumane (*inhumanus*) and should provide everything for the spiritual and corporal needs of the imprisoned.[13] Monks of the Third Order of the Franciscans of Strict Observance in Paris, who could be imprisoned for several years or even perpetually, were allowed to receive communion after one year of incarceration.[14]

An often quoted authority on monastic prisons was Antonius a Spiritu Sancto (1618–1674), a Discalced Carmelite of Portugal.[15] He stated that as long as the delinquent was not convicted of a crime or of trying to escape, his habit or tonsure could not be taken away and he should be permitted to celebrate Mass in an oratory next to the

11. Kober, "Gefängnisstrafe," 575–79.

12. *Regula Primitiva*, cap. 31, p. 4 (de carcere in nostrorum conventuum), 160–62. On the reading of spiritual books in early modern secular prisons, see Spierenburg, *Prison Experience*, 175–78.

13. *Constitutiones Fratrum Discalceatorum Beatissimae Virginis Mariae de Monte Carmelo Primitivae Observantiae Congregationis Hispaniae* (1787), part 4, ch. 4, 340.

14. *Regula et Constitutiones Fratrum Poenitentium Tertii Ordinis Sc. Francisi*, 132: "... incarceratis non, nisi post annum, administretur."

15. Antonius a Spiritu Sancto, *Directorium Regularium*, tract. 4, disp. 3, § 5, 77ff.

cell.[16] Even a convicted criminal could be allowed to celebrate Mass if he were truly repentant.[17] This, however,
was judicial theory and not practice. In 1787, the Spanish Carmelites stated that any monk who was sentenced
should be deprived of his hood, his scapular, his tunic, and
his tonsure.[18] In the hallway between the eight prison cells
of the Capuchins of Vienna, there was a little altar where
Mass was celebrated about five times a year and prisoners
could follow along through an opening in the doors. All
prisoners who refused to receive the sacrament of penance
were flagellated.[19] Some orders had provincial prisons for
hard-to-control cases—for example, the Franciscans and
Capuchins in Austria, the Franciscans of Venice and the
Carthusians. Especially rebellious monks or notorious
escapees were detained in places known for their secu-
rity, and due to this, the Regensburg Charterhouse held
monks from Spain (El Paular), Erfurt, and Danzig in the
seventeenth and eighteenth centuries. The prison there
was close to the monks' choir so that the prisoners could
follow the liturgy acoustically.[20] In the Charterhouse of

16. Ibid., num. 405, 77: ". . . imo ei permittitur missae sacrificium
quotidie celebrare in oratorio ad hoc iuxta carcerem . . ."

17. Ibid., num. 407, 78.

18. *Constitutiones Fratrum Discalceatorum* (1787), 341.

19. Allgemeines Verwaltungsarchiv Wien: Bestand Alter Kultus,
kath. Kirche 619, Sign. 63, Generalia, 339 ex 1783, Bericht of 19 February 1783, fol. 81–84v, signed Franz Karl Hägelin, Johann B. von
Zollern, Maximilian Stoll, and Friedrich Schilling. For the biographies
of these Austrian state employees, see Scherhak, "Klosterkerker," 96.

20. Stöhlker, "Kartause St. Veith in Prüll," 19. For the Franciscans
of Venice, see *Constitutiones Urbanae Ordinis Fratrum Minorum*,
298. The writing of love letters to nuns (*scribentes litteras amatorias
monialibus*) alone was a crime worthy of expulsion (299). A rare case
in which such love letters of religious—in this case, however, not to
nuns, but of a monk to his beloved—still exist is that of the Benedictine Bernhard Weinberger of Benediktbeuern in Bavaria. He was

Mauerbach near Vienna, there was a penitentiary chair on which monks could be tortured or punished, and all three prison cells were equipped with shackles, with one cell even containing a giant stone ball (weighing about four hundred pounds), most likely for torture purposes.[21] One member of the community was usually assigned to guard the prisoners, and if anyone died because of his negligence, he was excommunicated, but he also committed a mortal sin if he gave anyone illicit extras like food, drink, or ink and paper.[22] If someone escaped because of negligence or malice on the part of the guard, he himself was usually imprisoned or at least severely punished.[23] In the Capuchin monastery in Vienna, this assignment was called the "Lion's Guard" (*Löwenwärter*), which shows that many times prisoners were looked upon as dangerous animals.[24] In Poysdorf, the cell of the imprisoned Fr. Thuribius (d. 1806) was so filthy

sentenced to prison in 1753, not only for the love letters, but because he had sexual relations with two women; see Bayerisches Hauptstaatsarchiv München: Bayerische Benediktinerkongregation, Rubrik 48 Benediktbeuern, Nr. 6.

21. Scholz, "Kartause Mauerbach," 102; Boguth, "Aufhebung der Kartause Mauerbach," 301.

22. Sgroi, *Lux Praelatorum*, pt. 4, ch. 17, num. 36, 455.

23. *Constitutiones Fratrum Discalceatorum* (1787), 341. On prison guards in early modern prisons see again Spierenburg, *Prison Experience*, 105–34. It is remarkable that although it has been known for some time that authorities ran prisons according to paternalistic family models, hitherto nobody recognized that monastic institutions provided an additional insight into this model, since monks consider their order a family.

24. Allgemeines Verwaltungsarchiv Wien: Bestand Alter Kultus, kath. Kirche 619, Sign. 63, Generalia, 339 ex 1783, fol. 13–18 of 27 January 1783, at 13. This is the famous, anonymous letter written by the then-Capuchin Ignaz Fessler to Emperor Joseph II. In his memoires Fessler claims the letter was dated 24 February, a fact he must have misremembered (Fessler, *Rückblicke*, 93–97; ibid. also the traditional name for the prison guard).

(he loved to play with vermin) that the state commissioners feared the dirty walls and broken windows were not in the least "conducive to motivate" anyone to live "a happy life or to keep reason in command."[25] Things were not much better in the Franciscan holding cell in Paderborn in 1799.[26]

In defense of the Capuchins, it should be noted that Ignaz Fessler (1756–1839), a member of this order, acted as a whistleblower by informing the Austrian Archduke about their prisons despite state prohibition. Unfortunately, his appeal to Joseph II was a singular case:

> The feeling of humanity demands vengeance against these tyrants! Why does one not bring this priest [Thuribius] to a hospital where he could be helped? It is animal-like to beat him . . . half dead and then leave him without help for the rest of his life in prison . . . and all this is done by fellow priests . . . Where is Religion? Where is love for Humanity? Where is sympathy and mercy?[27]

The Vienna Franciscans even forced their penitents to climb down a rope into a well-like hole until the 1770s.[28] The Hebrew scholar Wilhelm Schickhard (1592–1635) therefore compared monastery prisons, not without a good dose of confessional polemics, to the prison caves in

25. Allgemeines Verwaltungsarchiv Wien: Bestand Alter Kultus, kath. Kirche 619, Sign. 63, Generalia, 339 ex 1783, Relation und Kommissions Protokoll of 4 February 1783, fol. 74. On Thuribius see also Scherhak, "Klosterkerker," 95f.

26. Becker, *Geschichte meiner Gefangenschaft*. Partly reprinted in Geismar, *Die politische*, 153–71.

27. Allgemeines Verwaltungsarchiv Wien: Bestand Alter Kultus, kath. Kirche 619, Sign. 63, Generalia, 339 ex 1783, fol. 13v.

28. Scherhak, "Klosterkerker," 86; Wiedemann, "Klosterkerker," 436.

ancient Palestine![29] Even the canonist Prospero Fagnani (d.
1678) wrote in his famous commentary on canon law that
he was appalled by the atrocious living conditions in French
ecclesiastical prisons,[30] and was even more disgusted by the
opinion of some canonists that a prelate could licitly starve
a damned member of his community to death. Instead,
Fagnani argued, such a superior, be he a bishop, abbot, or
prior, should be charged with homicide and stripped of his
office.[31] Even the famous Thomas Sanchez, SJ (1550–1610),

29. Schickard, *Jus Regium Hebræorum*, 59: ". . . quales etiam apud
monachos quondam in usu fuisse, ostendit locus quidam vicini coe-
nobii Bebenhusani . . ."

30. McManners, *Church and Society,* 1:196 is aware of prison cells
in Paris "in a tower in the first courtyard of the episcopal palace. In
all the eighteenth century, no one [layperson] was imprisoned in the
gaol of the *officialité* at Montpellier—a dark underground cellar in the
cloisters without a lock on the door." Cf. ibid., 197–98. In volume 2,
McManners gives some examples of grim state prisons—for example,
Pierre Encicse (2:378), where one was "incarcerated in a dark cell in
the rock, with a sordid latrine bucket emptied only once a week." See
ibid., 2:414–16 on the deposition and imprisonment of the Jansenist
bishop Soanen of Senez in 1727. A similar account is given for the
secular French prisons by the China missionary Francois-Regis Clet
(1748–1820), who therefore regarded the prisons in eighteenth-century China as much more humane: "In France I often heard of dungeons
and black-holes where men awaiting trial are confined in misery, so I
feel impelled to tell you something about the prisons in China, if only
to make Christians blush to be less humane than the Chinese in their
treatment of an unfortunate class" (Clark, *China's Saints*, 5).

31. Fagnani, *Commentaria,* decretalium, de verborum significa-
tione, novimus, 215–16: "Caeterum adverte, quia Officiales, qui con-
demnant Clericos in perpetuum carcerem non debent condemnatos
ponere in tali loco, vel carcere, in quo vivere non possint, sicut multi
carceres Episcoporum Regni Franciae pro Clericis de atroci crimine
damnatis, ubi non vivunt ultra sex, vel octo dies, quorum poena, seu
mors est gravior patibulo suspensorum, cum peiori, & duriori morte
magis languendo intereant. Et Officiales tali morte aliquos exponentes homicidiae, & irregulares reputantur: magis enim est afflictiva illa
mors, quae cum longiori languare sit. . . . Ex quibus etiam patet, quam

found it licit for a religious to escape from the monastery if he was unjustly interned and deprived of necessary food, water, and shelter.[32] Of course, there were always canonists, like the Austrian Leopold Pilati (1705–1755), who denied, most likely for apologetic reasons, the widespread accounts of power abuse in the cloister.[33] If Pilati was right that inhumane treatment, be it physical punishment or extremely bad living conditions in a prison, was an invention of anticlerical critics, then the passionate debate about such issues in early modern canon law would be all about a fictional reality, which is somewhat hard to believe.

The trend in the post-Tridentine Church to grudgingly accept the secular sovereign's jurisdiction with regard to civil crimes committed by members of the clergy was only brought about in central Europe due to pressure by

---

sit cavendum ab opinione quorundam modernorum, qui estimarunt, Praelatos Regulares posse damnare subditum, ut fame pereat in carcere, praecipiendo aliis subditis, ne cibos ei deferant." Ibid.: "Officiales tali morte aliquos exponentes homicidiae, & irregulares reputantur." On the responsibility of a prelate regarding an imprisoned monk (in the thirteenth century), see also Marmursztejn, "Issues obligatories," 79–80.

32. Sanchez, *Consilia seu Opuscula Moralia*, ii: lib. vi, ch. 4, dub. 11, 186: "Sit conclusio. Religiosi qui juste capti sunt, & in carcere, vel custodia suorum Praelatorum detenti, fugere non possunt, nec a talibus locis sibi praefixis exire. Ratio, quia per Religionis vota privarunt se naturali libertate, quam habebant fugiendi, & se obligarunt in castris ad voluntatem suorum Praelatorum manere. Ita . . . limitant Navar. & Salzedo cum licet poena carceris justa sit, at modus exeuendi est valde injustus, & a charitate Christiana valde alienus, & ibi proponunt exempla." One has to remark that most canonists did *not* concede this right to sustain one's life to female religious, because for them the vow of the cloister was considered stronger. Accordingly a nun could not even escape licitly if she had to fear death or mutilation (Pellizario, *Tractatio de Monialibus*, ch. 5, q. 22, num. 58–59, 128–29)!

33. Pilati, *Origines Juris Pontificii Ad Carolum Sextum* (Trient: 1739), lib. 5, tit. 10, 630: ". . . quodtamen numquam audivi . . ."

the state, as the abolitionist laws in Bavaria (1769), the Habsburg lands (1769/70), and Naples (1769) indicate.[34] Closing monastery prisons in Austria coincided with the introduction of a new penal system, the *Constitutio Criminalis Theresiana* of 1769.[35] For Joseph von Sonnenfels (1732–1817), the enlightened state reformer, the abolition was necessary in order to secure the state's supreme judicial authority in these matters. Monasteries that ran their own prisons not only violated this principle but were compared to seditious groups, such as a confraternity in Milan that required "blind obedience" of its members that bound them to silence if questioned by the sovereign.[36]

The accounts above relativize Owen Chadwick's remarks about the pleasantness of a monastery prison. He legitimately pointed to the fact that monasteries often punished people much more leniently than secular institutions, and that a regular argument against them was that they protected culprits from the rigor of the state, but he did not clearly distinguish what it meant to be a prisoner in a monastery as a layperson, versus as a monk. For the former, it could be quite pleasant to live in silence and attend liturgical services while keeping servants, but a monk was usually treated much worse because the prior or abbot had real authority over him, and because he was seen as a stain on the community's reputation.[37]

---

34. A well-documented trial against the Augustinian Pasquale Perez de Bivador in Naples (1757) brought about the end of monastic prisons in the kingdom of Naples. "Neuester Versuch, die Inquisition im Neapolitanischen einzuführen," *Le Bret's Magazin zum Gebrauch der Staaten- und Kirchengeschichte* 3 (1773) 160–95. Cf. Chadwick, *Popes and European Revolution*, 242–43.

35. Langbein, *Torture and the Law of Proof*, 50; Kwiatkowski, *Constitutio Criminalis Theresiana*.

36. Sonnenfels, *Grundsätze der Polizey*, i: num. 60, 77–80; num. 61, 80–83.

37. Chadwick, *Popes and European Revolution*, 241.

Our account above does not mean that all monasteries had dark dungeons, but clearly a lot of them did. Some orders and monasteries were more lenient, especially female orders and the reformed Benedictines in France, such as the monks of St. Maur or St. Viton. The Augustinian Sisters of S. Pierre Fourier stated in their constitutions that their prison was "a dark place, which is called *purgatory* or the correction room. It has to be safe and one should be able to lock it . . . but nevertheless it should be a healthy place, but . . . as far away from the dormitory of the sisters . . . as possible."[38] The Benedictine monks of St. Viton described their honorable prison (*custodia*) as a room that was bright enough for the reading of pious books, and was nothing like the dark underground prison in Vienna.[39] In the Benedictine congregation of St. Maur, the penitentiary was a regular cell much like the one in St. Viton, where wine was only withheld once a week. All other needs of body and mind were met so that no one fell into despair, and visitors were allowed with the permission of the superior.[40] It seems that only severe disciplinary cases were sent to the central prison on the romantic Mont-St. Michel, where sixteen monks were incarcerated around 1766.[41]

38. *Regel und Constitutionen*, 2:216: "Wann aber über alle diese angewende Bussen und Gebett. . . . jedoch nichts will verfangen und selbe in ihrer Bosheit verharren, ist noch übrig dass man sie einspörre in ein dunckles Orth . . ."

39. *Regula S. P. Benedicti et Constitutiones Congregationis SS. Vitoni et Hydulphi*, p. 2, sect. 1, ch. 17, 273: "cubiculum caute ibseratum, lucidum, salubre, in quo inclusi ad tempus semper determinatum, pios legant libros . . . et aliquos opus habeant perficiendum."

40. *Regula S. P. Benedicti et Constitutiones Congregationis S. Mauri*, cap. 22 (de culpis et poenis), art. 4, 193–200.

41. Chevallier, *Lomenie de Brienne et l'ordre monastique*, 1:195; Howard, *State of the Prisons*, 139. Howard also mentions the monastery prison of the Benedicti of Ghent: "Three dreary dungeons down nineteen steps: a little window in each: no prisoners. I went

The already mentioned Benedictine monks of St. Maur were not just more lenient when it came to punishing their members, but they can also be credited with having produced one of the first modern reflections on prison reform and the ways of resocializing wrongdoers.[42] These thoughts were put forth by Jean Mabillon (1632–1707) in 1695, yet only posthumously published in 1724.[43] Mabillon argued that whereas the state was more concerned with retribution and the restoration of order, ecclesiastical justice aimed at the welfare of the soul. Therefore, in monastery prisons the only means of punishment that should be employed were those conducive to such spiritual restoration.

> That is the reason why in the choice of punishments which the ecclesiastical judges should employ, the latter are obliged to prefer those which are most capable of filling the hearts of sinners with a spirit of compunction and penance . . . The justice practiced in monasteries against criminals should imitate the conduct of the Church and harshness should be banished from it. All should be paternal, since it is the justice meted out by a father to his son. Finally, the spirit of charity and mercy should preside above all in these judgments.[44]

For Mabillon, it was most important that the punishment was proportionate to the mental and physical

---

down; but my noting the dimensions of the windows etc. so enraged the Keeper that he would not indulge my curiosity any farther."

42. The following lines about Mabillon are taken from Lehner, *Enlightened Monks* (©2011 Oxford University Press), 105–7. I acknowledge with gratitude the permission of Oxford University Press to reprint this passage here.

43. Mabillon, "Réflexions sur les prisons." An English translation with commentary is provided by Sellin, "Jean Mabillon."

44. Sellin, "Jean Mabillon," 583.

capabilities of the criminal. Furthermore, charity demanded that a person's faults and crimes should not be publicized, not only to protect the criminal and the victim, but
also the religious house.[45] Another issue concerned the
day-to-day life of the prisoner himself. Normally, he was
totally separated from the community, could not receive
visitors, was not allowed to have books or to exercise any
occupation or labor, and in many cases was deprived of
attending Mass.[46] This, Mabillon observed, left the wrong-
doer without any spiritual or psychological assistance.
Therefore, prisoners should be allowed, within limits,
the opportunity to receive the sacraments and to read
books. It is quite remarkable how Mabillon stressed that
a superior should never be content with locking up one of
his monks, but should always seek to help him become a
member of the community again.

> All sorts of bodily remedies are used for sick
> monks, particularly those who have fallen into
> a lethargic state or some mental trouble; but for
> those whose souls have been struck by severe
> mortal maladies, one is content to throw them
> into a dungeon or to abandon them to them-
> selves, where they do not cure or rehabilitate
> themselves by their own efforts. Is there no fear
> that God will some day demand an account for
> the loss of their souls from the superiors who
> have thus neglected them?[47]

45. Ibid., 586.

46. Sellin, "Jean Mabillon," 588: "How can one support imprison-
ing people for several months or of several years without labor or
occupation? . . . What could a poor wretch do for days, weeks, or
years without consolation, spiritual aid or occupation? . . . Is it not an
almost insupportable temptation, infallibly ending in despair, insanity, or at least dejection?"

47. Ibid., 587.

The monastery prisons, as they were, served in the eyes of Mabillon no real purpose, especially if the inmates became insane, hardened, or desperate. According to the French monk, it would be better if first-time offenders were not tried in an ecclesiastical court of law, as long as their errors were not too grave, and all those who deserved a more severe punishment should first be subjected to labor and fasting. Moreover, prisoners should occasionally be allowed to go out for a walk. Mabillon also suggested that each order or province have a central correction facility, and the time spent in prison should not exceed six months. If monks were really incorrigible, they should be expelled or transferred to a different monastery, as long as they could attend to their duties there.

> There are other more useful and humiliating penances than imprisonment. Suspension from the order, inability to receive sacred orders, having the last place in the assemblies of the community, the privation of active and passive voice, and some extraordinary labors might, with respect to many, be more effective than prison.[48]

48. Ibid., 591.

3

Orders with
and without "Prisons"

Differences between Orders and Genders

THERE ARE SOME INTERESTING differences between religious orders with regard to the issue of prison and punishment. The Jesuits never had any monastic prisons, and most post-Tridentine orders like the Theatines, Barnabites, or Piarists no longer prescribed the administration of corporal punishment to their prisoners, with the notable exception of the Capuchins. Those that were only reformed after Trent (e.g., the Trinitarians), however, kept their ancient traditions of corporal punishment.[1] The Benedictines certainly had prisons, but never a detailed theory of punishment, as there were not many cases in which it was necessary. The

---

1. Kober, "Körperliche Züchtigung," 440, makes clear that the post-Tridentine orders condoned corporal punishment but only if it was self-inflicted.

Franciscan orders, however, developed an exhaustively detailed theory of criminal law and an abundance of works on the punishment of criminal confreres in early modernity, which was unique among religious orders.[2] Where does this difference stem from?

First, it seems that the Jesuits did not need prisons. According to Gregory XIV's bull *Ecclesiae Catholicae* of 1591, no. 14, the Jesuits had the same right as any other order to have prisons,[3] but they had extremely strict admission standards and rejection criteria for novices and could still expel members if needed.[4] Benedictines were usually very selective as well, especially because their vow of stability made it impossible to move a troublesome religious into a different monastery.[5] Most Franciscan orders, however, seem to have

2. *Constitutiones Societatis Jesu*, 2nd part (on dismissal). Incorrigible Jesuits were simply expelled after all other means of discipline, e.g., spiritual exercises, were exhausted.

3. *Magnum Bullarium Romanum*, ii:767–70.

4. Generally, men should be admitted only "if their fitness is in proportion to the extent to which they are endowed with both natural and acquired gifts of God, calculated to promote his service according to the purpose of the Society . . . let those who are admitted to be Coadjutors . . . be men . . . of good conscience, sedate, tractable, lovers of virtue and perfection, given to devotion; men, in their domestic and external conduct of edifying habits . . . who desire to serve . . . for the Glory of God."*Constitutiones Societatis Jesu,* 1st part, ch. 2, num. 2, 6. On rejection criteria, see ibid., 1st part, ch. 3, num. 1–16, 8–10.

5. For an example of the very basic admission criteria for the Franciscans, see Katzenberger, *Liber Vitae,* q. 2, 11. An example of Benedictine selectiveness is the sixteen-year-old noble girl Marianna von Eys, who was initially rejected in 1784 as novice by the abbey in Oberwerth in Coblenz, despite her sincere religious vocation, because of the blindness of her one eye and the likely blindness of the other eye in due time. Only for a much greater dowry and under pressure of the Archbishop of Trier did the abbess accept her. Landeshauptarchiv Koblenz: Best. 1 C, Nr. 19646, Abbes von Boyneburg to Archbishop Clemens Wenzeslaus of 23 July 1784. Cf. Lehner, *Enlightened Monks,* 27–30.

been happy to accept anyone who was healthy and had a general desire for virtue. This impression is buttressed by their general constitutions, with the exception of stricter standards in some provinces, such as the city of Venice. Broad studies on the social history of the Franciscans that could help verify this impression have not yet been done.[6] However, it seems that other orders may have recognized that being less discriminating led more easily to trouble, because the otherwise extremely hospitable Cassinese Benedictines forbade under punishment of excommunication (it is not clear whether the minor or major ban is meant) the reception of any mendicant into their monasteries.[7]

---

6. Excluded from admission to the order were, according to one document, criminals, former heretics, schismatics, and all those who were illegitimate children. Besides these negative exclusion criteria, however, the positive ones are relatively short. All who were received had to have a mild and modest temper, be gifted in mind or at least teachable, and healthy. Moreover, candidates had to have a desire to achieve virtue and be ready to obey, and finally, have impeccable morals. See *Constitutiones Urbanae Ordinis Fratrum Minorum*, 38–39; *Magnum Bullarium,* iii:144–47. For similar constitutions, see also *Statuta Provincialia*, 3–5. On illegitimacy as an impediment for priestly orders (in medieval times), see Landau, "Weihehindernis der Illegitimität in der Geschichte"; for illegitimacy as an impediment in monastic orders until about 1550, see Schreiner, "Defectus natalium"; for illegitimacy and dispensation from vows, see Schutte, *By Force and Fear,* 56, 70. The German and Bohemian Servites were especially careful not to accept friars who had syphilis; see Güntherode, *Römische Religionskasse,* iii:257: "In Ordinem nostrum non recipiantur morbo foedo gallico laborantes." On syphilis in early modern German hospitals, see Jütte, "Syphilis and Confinement."

7. Güntherode, *Römische Religionskasse,* ii: num. 17, 355. That the overall level of literacy among the Capuchins was as bad as the former Servite Karl von Güntherode (1740–1795) describes it is improbable, but his account of a Capuchin's answer in a theological exam—"I know nothing due to holy obedience"—seems not implausible (Güntherode, *Römische Religionskasse,* iii:261–62).

The varying admission requirements of the orders, however, are most likely not the only reason for this difference. Another probably had to do with the number of applicants. As the pool of applicants grew, so too did the number of religious who only grudgingly joined or had no real calling. While the Benedictines had a relatively stable number of members that did not increase much over time, the mendicants grew dramatically. The Capuchins had roughly twenty-seven thousand members in 1698, and by 1754 the order had almost thirty-three thousand. The Carmelites of Ancient Observance had some twelve thousand religious in 1700, but in 1788 that number had increased to fifteen thousand, while the Reformed Franciscans grew from twelve thousand members in 1700 to nineteen thousand in 1762.[8] Still, one might ask why the Jesuits and other post-Tridentine orders did not develop a differentiated penal system with harsh punishments as the Franciscans did. In the seventeenth and eighteenth centuries, society developed milder punishments for criminals that replaced harsher medieval practices as the crimes became less violent, and it seems as if most of the new religious orders followed this secular trend. Through post-conciliar reforms, they established a similar type of penal system that relied more on disciplinary measures and less on corporal punishment.[9]

Since the mendicant orders were founded in the Middle Ages and open to all applicants, they needed a penal system parallel to the secular one of the time, and while secular law developed and changed over time, their system of punishment stayed the same, and harsh medieval punishments were handed down for many crimes, such as slapping the prior. The post-Tridentine orders, however, were founded under

8. Schutte, *By Force and Fear*, 252.

9. Cf. the overview in Ruff, *Violence in Early Modern Europe*, 110–13.

different circumstances. All crimes had become less violent and consequently the punishments less harsh,[10] while at the same time a resurgent Catholic revival of monastic discipline slowly replaced morally deficient clergy with an increasingly educated, pious, and vocation-centered religious elite. Good evidence for this is that by 1677, most of the severe corporal punishments for clergy (*fustigationes*) had disappeared and were replaced with detention and correction facilities for diocesan clergy, as the contemporary Jesuit Ernricus Pirhing (1606–1679) testified.[11]

Finally, male and female orders also took different approaches to the subject of punishment and monastic prisons. Only male orders had a harsh penal system with handbooks on crimes and trial procedures, despite the fact that in 1750 there were 150,000 female religious.[12] One reason for this is that there were fewer and less atrocious crimes being committed in female convents, but this begs the question. It seems that early modern nuns were already socialized as girls to be more concerned with satisfying the needs of others instead of themselves, and this made them more motivated to live according to the rules and find fulfillment in the religious life. Moreover, this was often the only acceptable alternative to being married or becoming an old spinster. It was a way of life that was free from

10. Foucault, *Überwachen und Strafen*, 45; 93; 96–97; Ruff, *Violence in Early Modern Europe*, 73–117.

11. Pirhing, *Jus canonicum*, lib. 5, tit. 25, num. 1, 280: "Quanquam quae de percussione Clericorum, praesertim saecularium, statuta sunt, fere in desuetudinem abierint." For the statutes of the Norbertines and their differentiations of physical offenses, see Holsten and Brockie, *Codex Regularum*, v: ch. 8, num. 10, 285–86. See also Kober, "Körperliche Züchtigung," 68 for more evidence. For the history of correction facilities for diocesan clergy, see May, *Priesterhaus*; Struber, *Priesterkorrektionsanstalten*.

12. Beales, *Prosperity and Plunder*, 291.

overbearing husbands and the dangers of childbirth, yet steeped in service to others (e.g., in hospitals or schools) or if cloistered, by distinguished choir service. The fact that it was overwhelmingly men who asked for dispensation from their vows because of forced monachization buttresses this argument.[13] This also helps us understand why, for example, only one female convent in the Habsburg lands desired dissolution under Joseph II, and why most of these convents were shining examples of spiritual devotion, discipline, and harmony.[14]

13. Schutte, *By Force and Fear.*

14. See the excellent study of Ströbele, *Zwischen Kloster und Welt.* For example, Ströbele shows that the contemporary complaints against the monastery of Horber concerning regular visits of men were not about sexual relationships or bad discipline (ibid., 32–33). Contact with men was unavoidable since the nuns ran their own farm and employed male farm workers. The case of the Rottenburg nun Maria Anna Beck (ibid., 32, 40–41) is a rare exception. Beck had a longtime affair with a priest, delivered a child, and was transferred in 1777 to another monastery for her bad behavior. Archival material on her in the Hauptstaatsarchiv Stuttgart: B 38 I Bü 1144 und 1445, and the Diözesanarchiv Rottenburg: A I 2 c, Nr. 144, 145 and 146.

4

The Franciscan "Criminal Trial"

IT WAS PARTICULARLY THE challenge of medieval heresies that prompted canonists to improve existing criminal procedures and to invent "inquisitorial" trials. Regulations for early modern religious orders follow these canon law procedures and not secular law, which still lacked a proper methodology for dealing with crimes. The innovations of canon law were soon adopted and improved upon by secular criminal law, in particular in the Holy Roman Empire and its code of criminal law, the *Constitutio Criminalis Carolina* of 1532.[1] The religious orders, however, did not follow the independent development of secular criminal law but remained focused on their own canon law tradition.

The regulations of all branches of the Franciscan order made it clear that no friar was supposed to be incarcerated

---

1. Langbein, *Prosecuting Crime in the Renaissance*, 137, 140–212. On the church's influence on the development of the right of the modern state to inflict punishment, see Müller, "Einfluss der Kirche."

for minor offenses (*ob levam causam*) with the rigorous *carcer*, but only for major ones.[2] A prior who did not follow this rule, explained the Dominican Passerino in 1677, was excommunicated (major ban) by the force of the law itself (*latae sententiae*).[3] In 1769, an anonymous book appeared in Strasburg under the suspicious title *The Criminal Trial in the Franciscan Order*.[4] It soon became a best seller when numerous scandals about abuse in monastic prisons came to light that year.[5] Unlike many pamphlets against religious orders, however, this was an anthology of original sources,

2. *Constitutiones Urbanae*, 295. These constitutions give a detailed catalogue of how to correct friars and how to proceed in a criminal trial.

3. Passerino, *Regulare Tribunal*, q. 21, num. 13, 280. According to Sgroi, somebody who unjustly incarcerates a religious inflicts upon himself the major ban of excommunication; see Sgroi, *Lux Praelatorum*, pt. 4, ch. 17, num. 32, 454: "Carcerans injuste religiosum ipso facto excommunicationem . . ."; ibid., num. 33, 455: "Et carcer injustus esse potest quatuor de causis. Primo, ob defectum jurisdictionis & potestatis . . . Secundo, respectu personae, quae mittitur, quando est privilegata . . . Tertio, respectu causae, quia quando religiosus non est suspectus de fuga, opportet, ut constet prius de corpore delicti enormis, per quod infligitur poena corporalis a jure, & quod etiam sit constitutus post quam etiam sit constitutus postquam constet saltim semiplene de delicto, quando proceditur via accusationis, vel denuncationis, alos est injusta, ratione ordinis non servati . . . Quarto, respectu loci, in quo quis detinetur, quia carcer datus ad custodiam non debet teterimus, sed clarus, et humanus."

4. *Criminalprocess der Franciscaner.*

5. Philipp Wilhelm Freiherr von Linder wrote from Regensburg to the Archbishop of Mainz and Arch-Chancellor of the Holy Roman Empire on 16 January 1770 that the *Criminalprocess* was a best seller in the Free City of Regensburg, because people thought the previous year's case of the incarcerated nun Magdalena Paumann of the Munich Angerkloster would be illustrated in this book. Haus-, Hof-und Staatsarchiv Wien: MEA 72b, Letter of 16 January 1770, fol. 75ff. On Paumann, see Lipowsky, *Gemälde aus dem Nonnenleben*, and Anonymous, *Magdalena Paumann*.

comparable to the embarrassing translations of papal bulls and other church documents by the former Servite monk Karl von Güntherrode.[6]

In the following paragraphs I want to look more closely at the anonymous author's main Franciscan sources—namely Anaclet Reiffenstuel's (d. 1703) *Jus canonicum universum* (1714), Gaudentius van der Kerckhove's (d. 1703) *Methodus corrigendi Regulares, seu Praxis criminalis fratribus Minoribus propria omni regulari Judici accomodata* (1701), Ludovicus Maria Sinistrari de Ameno's (1622–1701) *Practica Criminalis* (1693), as well as his *Formularium Criminale* (1693).[7] The latter was used as a handbook by religious superiors and provincials when adjudicating criminal cases, and although an enormous variety of cases are listed, one should not assume that they were all invented. It seems more probable that the handbook existed in order to help deal with things like fistfights, assassination attempts with poison, theft, embezzlement, cooperation in abortions, and other matters, because these crimes were actually occurring.

While every monastery was regularly evaluated by other superiors of the order to assess the spiritual well-being of the religious house (*visitatio*) and correct any vices, this practice was in early modernity distinguished from official criminal trials.[8] Nevertheless, if such officials, called

6. Güntherode, *Römische Religionskasse*; Güntherode, *Römische Gesetzbuch*. Another anthology, written by a Protestant, is Eisenschmid, *Römisches Bullarium*.

7. Reiffenstuel, *Jus canonicum universum*; Kerckhove, *Methodus*. The anonymous author of the *Criminalprocess,* however, used the Cologne 1712 edition of Kerckhove, which was not accessible to me. Sinistrari, *Practica Criminalis,* 2 vols. The original *Practica Criminalis* of the Franciscan order was promulgated in 1639; Sinistrari comments on this earlier work. For Sinistrari, *Formularium Criminale,* the anonymous author used the 1754 edition.

8. *Criminalprocess der Franciscaner,* 12–17. Reiffenstuel, *Jus*

visitators, discovered sinful or criminal activity occurring within a monastery (e.g., heresy, sodomy, sacrilege, simony, counterfeiting, or conspiring against superiors), they could begin a trial in order to avoid further scandal and to deter others. They could also investigate rumors about alleged crimes being committed and then decide how best to handle them. For example, things like heterosexual fornication and adultery were serious offenses but were treated as *delicta privata* unless they caused a public scandal, in which case such offenses became *crimina excepta*.[9]

A criminal trial in a monastery was never a full "ordinary" trial as in a secular court of law, but a "summary trial." In a summary trial the regular or ordinary form of a trial, including the role of the judge, was modified according to the needs of a particular legal problem. In the case of a monastery this meant that the monastic setting, including its hierarchical structure, influenced how a trial was set up.[10]

---

canonicum, v: § 6 (De visitatione Regularium), fol. 26–29. Likewise, a superior does not have to follow the procedure for a trial for a simple paternal punishment of a religious (*poenae paternae*) (Hofmeister, "Vom Strafverfahren," 27).

9. *Criminalprocess der Franciscaner,* 17–20. Reiffenstuel, *Jus canonicum,* 5: § 7 (De process criminali), V, num. 309, fol. 30: "Si in visitatio ordinaria eidem etiam paterne tantum denuntiantur criminal excepta, vel publica, prout publicum opponitur private, quae videlicet in publicum detrimentum vergunt, qualia sunt: 1. Haeresis, 2. Crimen laesae Majestatis. 3. Blasphemia. 4. Crimen Sacrilegii, ut sortilegia, & prophanationes Sacrorum. 5. Latrocinium, & grassationes viarum publicarum. 6. Crimen Assassinii. 7. Crimen falsae Monetae. 8. Simonia . . . Porro in dicta nostra Practica Criminali pro ordine nostro Seraphico, inter criminal excepta, & publica insuper numerantur Conspiratio in Generalem, vel Provincialem, vel eorum Commissarios, aut etiam in Superiores locales; eorum item homicidia, vulnerationes, vel percussiones; item subornationes in electionibus . . . Item peccatis exceptis annumerantur Sodomia, & Sacrilegium cum Monacha. Item fornicatio, & adulteria . . ."

10. Danz, *Grundsätze der summarischen Prozesse,* 3–4.

Furthermore, a summary trial meant that the procedure was private, less rigorous, shorter, had its own rules, and most of all limited the possibility of defense—that is, the accused was not informed of what he was being accused of beforehand or who had testified against him, etc.[11]

Nevertheless, canon law required a more or less clear separation between the office of judge and prosecutor. The official charge had to be brought forward by an appointed prosecutor. A notary public had to be appointed, usually a monk, who acted on behalf of the prosecution by taking notes during interrogations and trial sessions. Furthermore, canon law required a legal counsel in defense of the delinquent. The defendant and the witnesses had to be questioned under oath. A sentence could only be publicized within the order if the guilty party confessed or was convicted, and all statutes of religious orders regarding criminal trials had to be followed.[12] Such a trial always included the possibility of judicial torture.[13]

A criminal trial began with either an accusation or an anonymous denunciation (private complaint procedure), or an inquisition (official investigation of the monastic superiors), unless a defendant was caught in the act of committing a crime. For example, if a religious blasphemed during a hearing, a formal accusation or inquisition became

11. Reiffenstuel, *Jus canonicum,* 5: § 7 (De processu criminali), num. 314, 30: "Processus Criminalis Regularium . . . non ordinarius, sed tantum summarius est, in eoque non nisi simpliciter, & de plano proceditur . . ." The idea of a *summary process* in secular law was born out of the intention to shorten long and complicated trials; see Sedatis, "Summarischer Prozess," in *Handwörterbuch der Rechtsgeschichte* 78–80; Hofmeister, "Vom Strafverfahren," 30.

12. Reiffenstuel, *Jus canonicum,* 5: § 7 (De processu criminali), num. 320, fol. 31.

13. Cf. Langbein, *Torture and the Law of Proof,* 49.

unnecessary.[14] If the trial began with an accusation, then a written statement (*libellum accusationis*) had to be given to the ordinary judge (*judex ordinarium*), who in the Franciscan order was the provincial, who then appointed (usually) the local prior as his delegate. The "definitors" of the Franciscan province, members of the provincial council, were considered real co-judges. After the judge was appointed, the defendant's testimony had to be heard, whether in person or in writing, and always under oath (*juramentum calumniae*). A notary public and two witnesses had to confirm with their signatures the written account of the hearing. If the defendant was extremely malicious and refused to cooperate, two additional assessors could be appointed to assist the judge. Accusations against superiors in good standing with the order did not have to be easily accepted *unless* another spotless monk brought them forth.[15] This privileged status of the superior explains the many unhappy endings of monastic trials; a superior could easily dismiss charges brought against him by defaming the accuser, who could then be locked up for conspiring against a superior

14. Reiffenstuel, *Jus canonicum,* 5: Tit. 1, § 8 (Compendiosa . . . Instructio practia rite formandi Processum Criminalem), num. 338, fol. 33; I, § 8, num. 547, 67: ". . . Si Reus in conspectu ipsius judicis. . . . peccat, v.g. blasphemat, Judicem percutit. . . ." On the difference between accusatorial and inquisitorial process, see Langbein, *Prosecuting Crime,* 129–39; Jerouschek, "Herausbildung des peinlichen Inquisitionsprozesses;" on denunciation in secular German law, see Koch, *Denunciatio,* esp. 57–66; 84–91.

15. *Criminalprocess der Franciscaner,* 25–34. On the formalities, see Reiffenstuel, *Jus canonicum,* 5: Tit. 1, § 8 (De praxi formandi processum), num. 340, fol. 34. On the creation of the notary, see ibid., num 344ff. On the possibility to dismiss accusations from monks of non-laudable character, etc., see Sinistrari, *Formularium Criminale,* sect. II, adnot. III, num. 25, 59: "Accusationes contra Praelato, & personas insignes non sunt recipiendae, nisi sint datae a Religiosis, de quorum zelo non ambigatur."

or for disturbing the peace. If a trial began with a denunciation, which was often anonymous, the procedure was the
same except for one major difference: the accuser did *not*
sign a statement of prosecution.[16] If a crime was committed
during the hearing itself, the sentence could be immediately
promulgated without further formalities.[17]

A good example of a trial by inquisition is the case
of the Franciscan Wendelin Heun (1730–1778), who
opted to join a different province after the secession of the
Thuringian Province but then decided, too late, to return
to his old one. The provincial of the Franciscans would not
allow this, and when Heun resisted and refused to obey
him, he was incarcerated for two years until the provincial
chapter began an official inquisitorial trial. During this
time, Heun frequently sent his superiors "impertinent" letters, threatening them with excommunication and never
conceding the sin of disobedience. The provincial definitors offered to ease his prison sentence if he recanted, but
only under pressure from the enlightened Archbishop of
Mainz, who had outlawed formal monastic prisons by 16
May 1770.[18] In 1771, when Heun was told he would be
permitted to make an appeal to the "definitors" of the province he wanted to rejoin, he rejected the offer and instead
requested to travel to Rome to sue the entire province. He
escaped while being transferred to a different monastery
and travelled to the Vatican, where the General of the order

16. *Criminalprocess der Franciscaner*, 38–55. Reiffenstuel, *Jus
canonicum*, 5: tit. I, § 8 (de praxi formandi processum per viam de-
nuntiationis), num. 534 ff., 65.

17. *Criminalprocess der Franciscaner*, 56. An example would be
that the accused committed an act of blasphemy during a hearing, or
an act of violence.

18. Plath, "Beispiel klösterlicher Jurisdiktion," 275–76. On the
drama of disobedience in female monastic houses in France, see Rapley, *Social History*, 49–62.

ordered the Franciscans of Thuringia to accept the mentally confused monk back into their community. The province, however, refused to do so, and instead apprehended and incarcerated Heun again in Sinsheim until his death in 1778. During his last weeks of life, the prior allowed Heun to be cared for by a physician in order to avoid the charge of negligent manslaughter and the consequent punishment of excommunication, but it was too late. According to the doctor's statements in the state-run investigation he initiated, Heun was kept in a dungeon without windows or heat and was often forced to subsist only on bread and water. The Franciscan ultimately died because his confreres withheld necessary medical treatment. His prior was exiled from the Palatinate after a few weeks of spiritual exercises under strict fasting.[19]

As in a secular criminal trial, one had to establish *corpus delicti*. For example, if a friar claimed to have been injured by someone in the order, a special judicial form laid out guidelines for how the wound should be inspected.[20] Physical harm was punished with the utmost severity, and not only among Franciscans. Even if the injured party wanted to excuse the assailant and protect his identity, the regulations of the Franciscans commanded him to reveal the attacker or be tortured![21] Once *corpus delicti* was estab-

19. When a state official inquired about the imprisoned monk during his lifetime, the prior lied and stated he would live in a different province of the order. Lying to state officials seems to have been a generally accepted policy, as one can see also from the scandals in Vienna in 1783. Plath, "Beispiel klösterlicher Jurisdiktion," 277–80.

20. *Criminalprocess der Franciscaner*, 61–62; Reiffenstuel, *Jus canonicum*, v: tit. I, § 8 (de visitatione corporis delicti), num. 356–59, fol. 36–37.

21. Sinistrari, *Formularium Criminale*, sect. III, 103f: "Forma examinandi Vulneratum . . . Si nolit revelare Vulnerantem ex timore, ne illi amplius noceat, aut etiam ex amore dicens Se illi agnoscere,

lished, the judge could move forward with the proceedings. In an informative process, the witnesses of the crime had to be questioned before the accused could be interrogated. The judge was required to refrain from leading questions, and the minute taker (*actuarius*) had to keep a record of their statements, which the witnesses later signed.[22] If one could not produce sufficient evidence to convict anyone (*indicium proximum seu remotum*), although it was apparent that a crime had been committed, one could allow a witness, who had been found guilty of being connected with the crime, to go unpunished if he revealed the identity of other guilty parties. Such a decree of immunity could only be drafted by the provincial, and it had to be published within the province and included in the files.[23]

---

ut bonus Christianus; & nolle, quod aliquam punitionem patiatur sui causa ille, qui eum vulneravit, debet moneri ut veritatem fateatur, quia alias peccat mortialiter, & erit Reus perjurii, nec sibi debet nocere in anima, ne proximo noceat in Corpore. Et debet non semel, sed bis, & ter moneri, & protestando illi, quod si non revelat, devenientur ad juris, & facti remedia, quibus revelare cogetur. Quod si persistat in contumacia non revelandi, ipse debet adigi per Torturam, ut manifestet Reum: & ipse debet adigi per Torturam, ut manifested Reum: & formam dabimus infra, quando dicemus de Testibus cogendis per Torturam. Et examen debet concludi clausula Paulo supra dicta; puta. Et lecta sibi prius sua depositione . . ."

22. Furthermore, it had to be established whether a witness was a *testis habilis*, a suitable and honorable witness. For this purpose he was asked general questions (*generalia*), e.g., whether he had received communion at least once in the previous twelve months, whether he had ever been excommunicated, etc. After this he was asked *specialia*; however, the judge was instructed not to begin by questioning the witness about the delinquent or his crime, but begin rather ambiguously and proceed slowly to a question about the crime. *Criminalprocess der Franciscaner*, 80–90.

23. *Der Criminalprocess der Franciscaner*, 92; Sinistrari, *Formularium*, sect. iv, num. XXIV, 141: "Forma concedeni impunitatem. Accidit aliquando, quod nullum potest haberi indicium. . . . delicto alioquin gravissimo patente, ob quod maximum damnum potest

Obtaining evidence outside the monastery was tricky because one could not launch an open investigation; this would have ruined the reputation of the order. Sinistrari's handbook contains a form for how to proceed in the case of a friar deflowering a virgin (*casu deflorationis*). In such a case the judge was supposed to engage a trustworthy midwife, who had to take an oath of absolute silence. She was supposed to visit the alleged sexual partner of the friar and physically examine her. The midwife had, according to Sinistrari, to be informed that her oath bound her to defend the good reputation of the girl and of the order. Thus, if somebody talked to her about the offense she had to lie and state that the rumor was a lie.[24] Such instructions, usually expressed orally, leave no record and seem not to have been taken into account by historians. Our awareness of their existence sheds a completely new light on the history of sexual behavior among clergy and goes a long way to explain the passionate denials of sexual misbehavior by religious superiors.

---

evenire Religioni. Tali casu, potest Provincialis solus (si periculum est in mora) impunitatem concedere Reo alicui, ut Correos revelet, dummodo nomine Generalis hoc faciat . . ." On the influence of canon law for the development of immunity for principal witnesses and on the evaluation of confessions, see Jerouschek, "Jenseits von Gut und Böse."

24. The anonymous editor of the *Criminalprocess* comments: "I have heard my entire life from the pulpit and in the confessional: You shall not commit a venial sin even if you could save the entire world from certain doom, and here the provincial commands the midwife to lie . . . in order to save the honor of the Franciscan Order!" (*Criminalprocess der Franciscaner*, 75). Sinistrari, *Formularium,* sect. III, num X, 107: "Quibus A. R. P., eam monuit, ut hoc sub secreto teneret, peccaret enim mortaliter, si proderet famam puaellae, & etiam, Religionis: imo injunxit, ut si aliquos audiret de hac re loquentes, dicat, se visitasse Puellam illam, & esse falsum, & sine fundamento, quod de ea dicitur. Et lecta sibi sua depositione, cum nollet aliquid addere, vel minuere . . ."

GATHERING JUDICIAL EVIDENCE THROUGH TORTURE

In a case in which no confession—the preferred means of conviction in a monastic trial—could be produced, the judges relied on witnesses to the criminal offense. For a case to be partially proved (*semiplene*), which was sufficient in a summary trial, only one reliable witness was necessary, and even a less reputable witness was adequate if his account was supported by other evidence. Even two twenty-year-olds could be such key witnesses, while a conviction with two witnesses of thirteen or fourteen years of age (*pubertatem egressus*) was only possible if others also supported their testimony. In addition, the testimony of a woman, young girl, or boy was satisfactory if the witness had a good reputation and the accused a bad one. Besides these, a number of other witness accounts could help prove a case partially—for example, even the rumor of a crime together with the bad reputation of the accused.[25]

If a reluctant witness denied having seen a crime although it was established that that he had witnessed it, the court could torture him to extract a confession. "Judicial torture"[26] was also applied if a witness contradicted himself in interrogations. It was used on a reluctant witness only if no other witnesses could be produced (*remedium subsidiarium in defectu aliarum probationum*). Nevertheless, Sinistrari advised that torture should be used preferably in order to force the accused to confess. Only in exceptional cases should witnesses be tortured, and if so, their physical

25. Sinistrari, *Practica criminalis,* 1: tit. 19, § 3, 661; *Criminalprocess der Franciscaner,* 139–40. For varieties of torture used by secular tribunals, see Langbein, *Torture and the Law of Proof.*

26. For the terminological difference between torture and punishment, see Langbein, *Torture and the Law of Proof,* 3; Garner, *Black's Law Dictionary,* 1498.

pain should be objectively much less than that of an accused religious.[27]

The German code of secular criminal law, the *Carolina* of 1532, followed this procedure, which is built upon an older canon law tradition, and also preferred coerced confessions of the accused over coerced witness accounts.[28] Enlightenment thinkers like Pierre Bayle (1647–1706) and Montesquieu (1689–1755), however, challenged the excessive use of torture for coercing confessions and argued for proportionality between crime and punishment. By 1764 also a few Catholic Enlighteners followed this new direction, most famously the jurist and philosopher Cesare Beccaria (1738–1794), who demanded in his 1764 *Dei delitti e delle pene* (*On Crimes and Punishments*) the abolition of torture and capital punishment and requested a more humane punishment for prisoners.[29] Only a few monastic theologians, like the erudite Augustinian Enlightener Jordan Simon (1719–1776), received Beccaria positively and consequently questioned the validity of torture in monastic criminal trials.[30] Therefore, secular authorities felt forced

27. *Criminalprocess der Franciscaner*, 95; 135.

28. Langbein, *Prosecution*, 179; 186–87; 273. While in the *Carolina* a judge's main source of evidence was torture, the French criminal law seems to have used it less often (ibid., 241): the French system ". . . has a professional prosecutor in charge of gathering evidence, who may have felt some pressure to do his job well enough to obviate the need for torture. The decision to torture is taken so seriously that the judge is obliged to put it to his legal advisory council. . . . These are grounds for believing that French practice may in fact have been somewhat less torture-prone than German, despite the greater concern of the German legislation with safeguarding the rights of the accused" (ibid., 241).

29. Rother, "Zwischen Utilitarismus und Kontraktualismus."

30. Simon, *Institutiones Canonicae*, lib. 4, tit. 2, 1122–34; tit. 3, 1134–40; tit. 4, 1140–47. On the change of judicial thought regarding torture, see Langbein, *Torture and the Law of Proof*.

to act on behalf of inhumanely treated religious. In the Habsburg lands one of the leading theorists who led the charge against monastic prisons and monastic sovereignty was the political scientist Joseph Wiener von Sonnenfels (1733–1817), who had achieved the abolition of judicial torture in secular Habsburg courts in 1776.[31] The passionate attacks of judicial reformers like Sonnenfels are quite understandable if one considers that religious orders kept following canon lawyers like Sinistrari, and not the enlightened voices of their orders, like Simon.

Sinistrari gave in his *Practica Criminalis* a rationale for the torture of witnesses, relying on the General Statutes of the Franciscan Observants for the cismontane families of the order. However, it condoned the practice of inflicting pain and physical coercion only for atrocious crimes—that is, as corporal punishment of the *convicted criminal*—but did not mention witnesses. This shows a lack of differentiation between torture as the use of physical coercion (the infliction of pain to extract a confession or testimony) and painful corporal punishment. The modes of corporal punishment described here could be used for torture:

> Painful punishment [*tortura*] should only be inflicted for atrocious and severe crimes. Since it is not sufficiently known how one should torment [*torquendi*] criminal friars, we command that if the crime is abominable [*nefandum*], the friar should be tortured with fire. In the remaining other cases one should torture the delinquent naked, and with his hands bound, three times, according to the decision of the superior

31. On Sonnenfels, see Cattaneo, *Aufklärung und Strafrecht*, 49–53; Beales, *Joseph II*, 529–30; 548, 655. On the abolition of torture in Europe, see Schmoeckel, *Humanität und Staatsraison*, 69–70, 178–86. On the abolition of monastic prisons in the Habsburg lands, see chapter 3 of this book.

> with flagellations, and let him fast at water and
> bread. If the crime was atrocious [*atrox*], then
> the judge, who by law investigates the case, can
> apply a different torture according to his own
> arbitrary decision . . .[32]

Sinistrari insisted in his commentary that physical punishment (e.g., flagellation) should not be longer than twice the length of reciting psalm 51. However, such chastisement was according to him no longer in usage in Italy, but still in force in the provinces "ultramontanis," that is from his perspective north of the Alps, as well as in Naples. Similar chastisements were used to "treat" the insane religious, or whoever the superior considered as such. An extreme case is that of the Servite Candidus Maria Baldhauser, who was imprisoned in the monastery of his order in Prague in 1783, ten years after Joseph II had made such treatment illegal. Since he wished to leave the order because he felt he had been pressured into taking vows, his back was inflicted with three big blisters, which soon developed maggots, and other painful punishments. The superior insisted Candidus was insane, while his parents stated he just wanted to leave the Servite Order. The actions of the

32. Sinistrari, *Practica criminalis illustrata,* i: tit. XVI, 580–81: "Tortura pro atrocibus, & gravioribus delictis, dumtaxat infligenda est. Verum cum non satis constet, quomodo torquendi sint Fratres delinquentes, decernimus; quod si crimen sit nefandum, ignis poena rei torqueantur: de reliquis vero criminibus suspecti, nudi, & manibus ligati, per tria intervalla, flagellis, Superioris arbitrio, dire torqueantur, ac pane, & aqua macerentur. Quod si crimen atrox fuerit, iudex ad quem cognitio causae quovis iure pertinet, aliud torturae genus, arbitrio suo, iuxta qualitatem delicti, excogitare possit." Cf. Sambuca, *Constitutiones et statuta generalia cismontanae familiae Ordinis Sancti Francisci,* ch. 7, § 17–18, 73. A "crimen nefandum" was usually sodomy. In all orders sodomy was punished with perpetual confinement; for example, in the Norbertine order, see Holsten and Brockie, *Codex Regularum,* v: ch. 8, num. 9, 283.

superior were illegal according to canon and state law, but even his parents could not free their son or save him from life-threatening treatments like extreme bloodletting. Whether he survived these we do not know.[33]

No secular person (*neque per laicos saeculares posset administrari similis tortura*) could ever inflict painful punishment on a religious.[34] Only the provincial could impose such punishment after close study of the process files, careful deliberation, and consultation with the definitors of the province. The provincial was, however, allowed to circumvent the definitors and instead to ask members of the order in exceptionally good standing to advise him.[35] *Arctatio*, that is confinement, combined with flagellation and fasting, was the most common punishment. Flogging could not be longer than three *Miserere* (Ps 51). While confined, the delinquent was not to be told how long his imprisonment would last. During this time he should fast three times a week with a diet of bread and water and whip himself once a week in the refectory in front of the community, with his hands tied, and naked except for a piece of linen covering his genitals. While regular confinement could happen in one's cell, the qualified *arctatio* happened in a penitentiary (*domus disciplinae*).[36] For more atrocious

33. Allgemeines Verwaltungsarchiv Wien: Bestand Alter Kultus, kath. Kirche 619, Sign. 63, Mähren und Schlesien, 3 ex November 1783, letter of Wolfgang and Rosalia Baldhauser of 14 September 1783.

34. *Criminalprocess der Franciscaner*, 98–99; Sinistrari, *Practica criminalis*, 1: tit. XVI, 581.

35. *Criminalprocess der Franciscaner*, 100–101. Sinistrari, *Formularium*, sec. VII, num. I, 292–93.

36. Sinistrari, *Practica criminalis illustrata*, 1: tit. XVI, § 2, 583: "In gravioribus delictis arctatione, flagellis, jejuniis, taxillis, vel sibilis iudices uti permittuntur. Itaut de medacio, vel de crimine, suspecti nudi, cum solis femoralibus manibus ligati, per tria intervalla flagellis superioris arbitrio dire torqueri possint; et pane et aqua macerari;

crimes, ankle screws (*per taxillis*) or finger screws (*per sibilis*) could be temporarily added. These two kinds of torture were extremely painful and were supposed to last no longer than one hour altogether, and were not supposed to be repeated more than three times: the first time fifteen minutes, the second time half an hour, the third time a whole hour. By *sibilis* one understood little pikes usually made of iron or polished wood. They were placed between digit, middle, and ring fingers, connected by a band. The stronger the band was pulled together the greater the pain. By the punishment *per taxillis* one understood the application of little dice, made out of animal bones, which were then pressed on the joints of the delinquent with the help of a wooden screw (in Italian, *la stanghetta*).[37]

For physical chastisement beyond confinement, the commentators on Franciscan law advise the prior to consult a secular lawyer and to ensure the presence of a physician so that the delinquent would not die during the painful treatment. The same advice applied when torture was used to extract a confession or witness testimony.[38] The harshest punishment was the fire torment, which was supposed to last no longer than six minutes.[39] The suspect had to sit in the middle of the room with bare feet, which were emulsified in pork fat. Then a pot with glowing coals was put a hand's length away from his feet. In 1693, Sinistrari

idque bis vel ter replicari, prout ratio suaserit. Arctatus nesciat tempus, in quo ter in hebdomada in pane & aqua jejunare debet, et sibi disciplinae flagella in publico Refectorio infligere unius *Miserere mei* & c. spatio." Cf. *Criminalprocess der Franciscaner*, 108–10.

37. Sinistrari, *Formularium*, sect. VII, num. XI, 302–3. For an illustration of a legscrew, see Langbein, *Torture and the Law of Proof*, 25–26.

38. Sinistrari, *Formularium*, sect. VII, num. XI, 302–3. *Criminalprocess der Franciscaner*, 111–19.

39. *Criminalprocess der Franciscaner*, 131.

already called this torture too gruesome and therefore out of practice; even secular law had long abandoned it.[40] In Genoa, a prior—it is not known at what time and also no source is indicated—came up with the idea of tormenting an assassin with hot hardboiled eggs that were put under the shaved arm pits of the delinquent, while his arms were pressed against his body for the length of the Nicene Creed. Sinistrari praised this punishment as the most "exquisite" and least harmful one, but he recommended it nevertheless only for the most atrocious cases.[41]

THE QUESTIONING OF THE ACCUSED

Only once a case was partially proved (*semiplene*) was the suspect called to the stand.[42] It was crucial that the accused had to be heard in court, otherwise he could not be

40. *Criminalprocess der Franciscaner*, 124; Sinistrari, *Formularium*, sect. VII, num. XXIX, 316: "Forma Torquendi per Ignem. Tortura Ignis. . . . antiquitus ita exercebatur. Reus compeditus, & manicatus, sedebat in plano camerae tormentorum, nudatis pedibus; mox plantae pedum ungebantur lardo porcino; subinde patella ferrea plena prunis ardentibus approximabatur ad distantiam palmi unius, cum dimidio, sicque pedes exustulabantur, itaut intolerabilis causaretur dolor. Sed tortura haec, ut nimis barabara, & periculosa, antiquata est . . ."

41. *Criminalprocess der Franciscaner*, 125; Sinistrari, *Practica criminalis*, 1: tit. XVI, § 1, num. 5, 581: "Et audivi aliquando, quod Genuae quidam judex regularis procedens in casu atrocissimi assassinii . . . Certe exquitissimum (& forte tale, acrius non puto dari salvo corpore) fuit tormentum hoc & non periculosum, praeter enim actualem dolorem . . . nihil relinquat in corpore, praeter modicam inflammationem, cui facile potest linimento refrigeranti subveniri . . ."

42. Sinistrari, *Practica criminalis*, 1: tit. XIX, § 3, num. 10, 660: "Reus non constituendus ante semiplenam probationem delicti. Indicia aequipollentia semiplenae probationi sunt indicia gravia. . . . Reus non tenetur respondere judici, si delictum non est prius semilene probatum. Et judex mortaliter peccat."

sentenced. If there was danger of escape, the suspect could be incarcerated. If he escaped successfully, other monasteries had to be informed and had to return the suspect immediately.[43] If a monk did not appear in front of the judge, he could be declared stubborn or disobedient (*contumax*) and excommunicated (major ban). If he was then found and arrested, he had to first receive absolution in order to be examined and sentenced. With the pronunciation of the sentence he was again excommunicated.[44] If a delinquent did not flee, he faced the judge, who admonished him to answer truthfully since he was under oath. Reiffenstuel argued in his commentary that the judge could tell the accused that all his crimes had already been proven beyond doubt, even if it was not true, and that he would find a much more merciful judge if he confessed.[45] If the suspect proclaimed his

43. *Criminalprocess der Franciscaner*, 140–51.

44. Sinistrari, *Practica criminalis*, 1: tit. XIX, § 7, 675: "Reus citatus, nec comparens declarandus est contumax." Ibid., § 9, 683: "Reus repertus excommunicatus prius absolvi debet, quam ulterius examinetur, ad effectum se sistendi in judicio; quo elapso, in eandem excommunicationem reincidit, a qua iterum absolvi debet, ut celebrare possit. Nisi is, qui judicat, sit suus superior Ordinarius, qui semel illum complete absolvat."

45. Reiffenstuel, *Ius canonicum*, Tit. I, § 7, num. 406, 43: "Si Reus nondum fugit, sed citatus comparet, et constituitur coram judice, debet hic ante omnia charitative reum admonere de statu suo, videlicet, quomodo ut legitime constitutus Reum compareat, debet ipsum adhortari debite, & imponere illi juramentum de dicenda veritate: Adhortatio praecipue fieri potest de obligatione sub mortali peccato duplici tam contra obedientiam, quam contra religionem (contra quam perjurando ageret) sincere in omnibus fatendi veritatem, & ad sensum judiciis sine aequivocatione, aut restrictione mentali respondendi: In eadem adhortatione praemonere poterit, quod nisi in cunctis sincere & veridice respondeat, brevi temporis spatio plurima sit non mussurus perjuria . . . indeque causam sibi duriorem faciat . . . Praecipue autem debet ei intimare, quod delictum, vel delicta, de quibus interrogabitur, sint taliter in actis probata, ut judex

innocence and instead of answering the questions of the judge, which had to be nonsuggestive,[46] desired to see the list of accusations or the list of witnesses, the judge was not supposed to comply with his wishes, because this would have enabled him to answer the explicit charges and thus to give a viable defense (*facile praeparare se posset ad respondendum*). From the autobiographies of accused monks we know, however, that one could reconstruct the charges once one heard the questions of the judge.[47] If an accused religious was called several times to testify, he had to take an oath each time—and was to be admonished the third time that a lie under oath would lead to perpetual confinement. As one commentator concedes, this could easily be abused. A superior convinced of the falsity of a statement could call the monk three times in order to justify the perpetual imprisonment of the monk. One could argue that such a prior materially contributed to a mortal sin, namely, blasphemous perjury.[48] These problematic procedures demonstrate that the trials often must have been mockeries of justice, rather than real attempts to uncover the truth.

ipsum legitime interrogare, & consequenter reus ad interrogationes sub obedientia, sub culpa, ac poena perjurii respondere teneatur." This reminds one of the interrogation methods of the *Malleus Maleficarum* in wichcraft trials; see Decker, *Witchcraft and the Papacy*, 66.

46. *Criminalprocess der Franciscaner*, 166–97. Cf. Sinistrari, *Practica criminalis*, 1: 1, tit. XIX, § 4, num. 17–23, 662–68.

47. Reiffenstuel, *Ius canonicum*, § 7, num. 407, 44; *Der Criminalprocess der Franciscaner*, 155–56; for several such reconstructions—the monk found out about the charges only through the final verdict—see Oehninger, *Wölfe in Schaf-Kleidern*. The German *Constitutio Criminalis Carolina* of 1532 also forbade suggestive questioning (under torture); see Langbein, *Torture and the Law of Proof*, 5, 1; also Langbein, *Prosecution*, 183.

48. *Criminalprocess der Franciscaner*, 192.

LEGAL DEFENSE FOR THE ACCUSED

Accused members of religious orders had, as in similar trials under canon law, the right to a defense counsel. This
was a remarkable right given the fact that defense counsel
for felony or treason charges was prohibited in English
common law until the eighteenth century, and rejected in
the French ordinance of Villers-Cotterets of 1539.[49] In a
monastery trial, such an *advocatus* had to be a member of
the order so that the trial records would remain secret.[50]
Only in extreme cases could a friar-counsel ask a secular
lawyer for advice; a judge could consult a secular jurist if
the accused could be punished with galley service, prison,
or painful punishments. Likewise, a lawyer's services could
be employed if a monk-judge did not feel judicially com-
petent enough to conduct a trial. In such a case, the canon
law commentaries advised that the judge should follow the
recommendation of the lawyer. Apart from these two cases,
a judge or advocate could never approach secular help
without becoming guilty of revealing the secrets of the order, which in itself was a serious offense.[51] The legal counsel
of the defendant, just like in secular law, did not have to

49. Langbein, *Prosecution,* 77–78, 233, 235–37; Langbein, "Prosecutorial Origins of Defence Counsel"; Beattie, "Scales of Justice."

50. *Criminalprocess der Franciscaner,* 205; Reiffenstuel, *Ius canonicum,* Tit. 1, § 8, num. 441: "advocatum ex Ordine."

51. *Criminalprocess der Franciscaner,* 206–7. The text quoted on
these pages is not from Reiffenstuel as claimed ibid. but from Sinis-
tratri, *Practica criminalis,* 1: 1, Tit. XX, § III, 710: ". . . poterit patronus
peritum, aliquem, devotum, ac secretum saecularem adire pro consilio. . . . His duobus casibus exceptis, tam Patronus, quam Judex, qui
ad saeculares fratrum causas, pro consilio, vel auxilio, quoquomodo
detulerint, revelationis secretorum ordinis poenas incurrisse, statua
declarant." Ibid., num. 24, 711.

swear in his oath before the judge to do the best he could to
defend his client.[52]

Despite the clearly codified right to legal counsel, a superior could find a way to sabotage a successful defense. The
case of Mansuet Oehninger (1713–1778), a Capuchin from
Würzburg, Germany, is illustrative. Since he did not appear
three times at a hearing in 1753, in which he was accused of
disturbing the peace in the province of Franconia and caus-
ing scandal by criticizing the financial bearing of his order,
he was declared *contumax*, which robbed him of his right
to any defense in trial, and he was immediately imprisoned.
Two years later, following his liberation from prison, he was
tried for arson. This time he could choose defense counsel,
but no friar was experienced enough or willing to speak up
against the provincial, who held a grudge against Oehninger. Later during the trial, his counsel was suspended because of direct contempt of court; Oehninger was declared
contumax and sentenced to prison.[53] Since he appealed, his
sentence was doubled.[54]

Santoro de Melfi, one of the most celebrated seventeenth-century Franciscan canonists, confirms that it could
be hard or almost impossible to get justice once one was incarcerated, because a prior could not be incarcerated unless
the notoriety of his crime was evident, and because an incarcerated monk could *only* be liberated by decree of the provincial.[55] This certainly gave the prior somewhat dictatorial
powers. That such misgiving was indeed warranted one can
see from the case of Fr. Anianus Horn (1683–1750) of the
Capuchins in Bamberg, Germany. Horn served as professor
of theology and philosophy in his monastery, lecturing the

---

52. *Der Criminalprocess der Franciscaner*, 217–27.

53. Oehninger, *Wölfe in Schaf-Kleidern*, 220–29.

54. Ibid., 234–35. He was sentenced to four months in prison.

55. Melfi, *Poenalium*, pt. 1, ch. 4, 167.

young students of his order. He was appalled by the policy of the Capuchins to acquire and invest money, and accused the provincial of breaking the rules of poverty in a letter he addressed in 1720 to the General of the Order in Rome. Oehninger reports that the General commended Horn for his communication and asked him to collect more evidence about such abuses so that proper reforms could be initiated. His provincial in Franconia, however, proscribed this investigation. Horn felt obliged by his conscience to follow the General's order and proceeded to investigate, with the result that he was incarcerated one night as "stubborn" and disobedient. Thus he was not given the chance to defend himself in a trial but was simply locked up in 1721. Since he was a well-known figure in the city of Mergentheim, he was moved to the prison of the monastery in Ochsenfurt, where he was flagellated twice a day.[56] At some point—and the sources differ here, suggesting either 1726 or 1736—the prison guard left the door unlocked and Anianus escaped over the garden wall. He first went to his home town, Karlstadt, where his family was well regarded, and then travelled with the help of the local priest to Würzburg to accuse the monks in person to the auxiliary bishop Johann Bernhard Mayer (r. 1704–1747). According to Oehninger, he escaped twice and appealed twice in person to the bishop, who handed him over each time to the Capuchins, since the order was exempt from his jurisdiction.[57] All accounts agree that Horn was from then on imprisoned in Würzburg in a dishonorable prison, declared infamous and subject to corporal punishment until his death in 1750.[58] Only before

56. Oehninger, *Wölfe in Schaf-Kleidern*, 16–28.

57. Ibid., 29–33.

58. Ibid., 44. Oehninger seems to refer to Habsheim, *Summula selectarum questionum*, sect. V "electio", additio num. 166, 463:" . . . ex detrusione in carcerem, ex privatione officiis ac dignitatis, ex

his death, which seems to have been the consequence of an extreme whipping, was he given the opportunity to confess his sins and to receive communion, for the first time since 1724. Oehninger reports that he rejected it.[59] Thus, the account that he was buried under the garden compost and not in holy ground—because he was an unrepentant excommunicated sinner—seems trustworthy. If one moreover takes into account the rage that was stirred up if a monk rejected confession and communion, it also becomes believable that it was not found necessary to make a replacement for the lost key to open his chains, but rather cut off his hands and feet, as a contemporary source claims.[60] A letter to the editor of a Franconian journal, written by a definitor of the Capuchin province of 1791, admitted to the burial in the garden, but claimed that a regular burial in the crypt would have caused a public scandal, and even conceded that the key to Horn's chains had been lost and that one had to break them open. The charge, however, for unjust imprisonment was rejected. Instead, the order claimed that Horn was insane and received proper and gentle care.[61]

At first sight this account, presented by the ex-monk and confrere of Horn, Oehninger, seems to be typical

---

dejectione a gradu professionis & apud nos ex delatione Caparonis. Denique toties, quoties publica poenitentia per judicis sententiam alicui judicaliter imponitur . . . In modo procedendi reformato novissime n. 108 declarantur infames, perjuris vel qui de haeresi suspecti abjuraverunt, de furto convicti aut de crimine pessimo, apostata a religione, qui in judicio contra aliios falsum testimonium dixerunt, malefici, falsarii litterarum, manus aut sigilli superioris, & qui condemnati fuerunt tanquam infamatores."

59. Ibid., 54.

60. Anonymous, "Trauriges Schicksal des P. Anianus." The biographical dates for Anianus Horn are taken from a letter to the author from the Provincial Archives of the Bavarian Capuchins dated 7 November 2011.

61. Anonymous, "Widerlegung der Fabel von P. Anian."

anti-monastic literature—too gruesome to be believed by a critical historian. One is tempted to trust the reply of other Capuchin witnesses in a different journal, which stated that Horn was insane and was treated extraordinarily well and never whipped, but what other response would one expect from the order?[62] The rules of the order forbade any concessions that could harm its reputation—one had to "bend" the truth. Yet, an independent source, the chronicles of the Cathedral vicar Johann Andreas Geissler (1705–1779), supports most of Oehninger's claims; only the dates in the accounts differ. Most importantly, Geissler confirms that the old Capuchin was imprisoned not because of insanity or visions, as some pretended, but because "he taught a proposition" and was not willing to remain silent about it out of obligation to his conscience. Moreover, he confirms that "the good and honest" Anianus Horn, after the escape from Ochsenfurt, went to the auxiliary bishop and was, because of the wounds inflicted upon him, not able to walk and so had to be carried in front of him. He also confirms that such punishments had been inflicted by a tyrannical superior, that they were disproportionate and unjust, and that Horn had been detained not in a bright, sunny room, as the Capuchins wanted the public to believe, but in a windowless, unheated dungeon.[63] The account of the imprisonment of Linus Hasse in a number of Westphalian Capuchin monasteries in the last decades of the eighteenth century paints a similarly dark picture of monastic prisons in this order.[64]

62. Anonymous, "Beleuchtung der vorgeblichen Bestättigung der Geschichte des Pater Anians."

63. Staatsarchiv Würzburg: HV Ms. f. 205 (Chronik des Johann Andreas Geisler), fol. 52–52r.

64. Hasse, *Klosterzwang und Klosterflucht.*

VERDICTS, SENTENCES, AND APPEALS

The sentence was either absolution or condemnation. The judge in a monastic "criminal" trial was for mendicants the provincial or his delegate, together with the definitors of the province; for Benedictines, the abbot. Both delinquent and counsel had to be present at the promulgation of the sentence.[65] On 12 April 1753, the abbot of Benedictbeuern in Bavaria sentenced the monk Bernard Weinberger (1711–1793) to prison. The Latin explanation of the sentence is five pages long and shows that the Benedictine order followed procedures similar to those of the mendicants.[66] It states that the punishment was the result of a proper inquisitorial trial. In the name of the Holy Trinity the monk was sentenced by the abbot as proper judge (*judex ordinarius*), after consultation with all other monks, for planning "total" apostasy, as well as three previous cases of apostasy from religious life; for uttering heretical propositions and teaching them to children and young adults; for superstition and magic; for fornication with two sisters (*de lapsu carnis cum duabus sororibus*); for love letters and other grave violations—for example, the violation of the cloister (*violationae clausurae*) by letting women stay overnight in his cell; for the threat of arson; for hitting the monastery hunter (*percussionem*); for breaking the vow of poverty; for possession of weapons (*arma clam in cella detenta*); for attempting to escape during his trial; and for sacrilege, because he absolved in the confessional the woman with whom he had intercourse. Weinberger could bring nothing else to his defense than allegations and perjury, and finally confessed since the prosecution had mature and trustworthy

65. *Criminalprocess der Franciscaner*, 231; Sinistrari, *Practica criminalis*, 1: tit. XXI, § IV, 770; Reiffenstuel, *Jus canoncium*, 5: § VIII, tit. I, 60.

66. Hauptstaatsarchiv München: Bayerische Benediktinerkongregation, Rubrik 48 Benediktbeuern, Nr. 6.

witnesses for all of his offenses. For apostasy and heresy he was sentenced to perpetual imprisonment in his cell, with one leg manacled in order to prevent (*procavenda*) future maladies and scandals. Moreover, according to the document, he had to be regarded until his death as incorrigible so that nobody could change his sentence or pardon him. For the crimes of fornication and desecration of the cloister he was sentenced to endure until his sixtieth birthday strict fasting (bread and water only) on the fourth and sixth day of the week. On high feast days even the wine was supposed to be withheld. From his sixty-first year on he was able to receive regular food as to quantity and quality. For the sin and crime of sacrilege, for the intentions to marry and to burn down the monastery, he was declared excommunicated (*excommunicatione majori*) and lost all election rights in the community. The sentence was read and published (*publicata*) in the monastery and was signed by the abbot, two assessors, the *actuarius* or notary public, and two witnesses.[67]

An appeal against a verdict was possible, but only within ten days after the promulgation; otherwise it was considered null and void.[68] Nevertheless, the appeal was often enough an absurdity, since one could only appeal to the next higher superior in the order—in the case of the Franciscans or other mendicants the General in Rome, who was not very likely to overturn a sentence because the local superior was usually considered more qualified to judge an individual, and individuals who felt that their rights had been violated were distrusted.[69] Even the Franciscan canonist Sinistrari conceded that because superiors appointed

67. Weinberger was later pardoned and was, at least from 1771 on, once again a monk in good standing with his community. See Hemmerle, *Benediktinerabtei Benediktbeuern*, 653–54.

68. *Der Criminalprocess der Franciscaner*, 242.

69. Ibid., 242–43.

their friends to judicial offices, one could not expect justice if one appealed to the provincial or General.[70] Moreover, a local superior could easily sabotage an appeal by declaring it frivolous (*appellatio frivola*), forcing its rejection and the punishment of the appellant with a doubling of the original sentence. Appeals to the sovereign were considered frivolous in most orders, the Theatines and Somaschi being the exceptions.[71] A good example of such a proscription of the *recursus ad principem* are the statutes of the Carthusians, which forbade it under punishment of lifelong imprisonment and excommunication. When the Habsburg court learned about this statute from government employees in Freiburg im Breisgau, who had discovered it by accident despite the fact that it had been printed generations earlier, the dowager empress Maria Theresa issued immediately a decree on 20 December 1779 for all her lands, in which she condemned such rules as an infringement upon her rights as sovereign.[72] The Servites, who had a similar regulation,

70. Sinistrari, *De delictis,* tit. 2, § 3 (Applicatio mala), num. 23, 62: "Aliquoties, et ut in pluribus, provinciales localium, et generales provincialium superiorum partes, quamvis contra justitiam, tuentur; exuuntque indifferentiam patris, ac judicis, ac induunt personam, ac partialitatem colligantis; et tunc quomodo ab his speranda justitia, aut contra oppressionem levamen? . . . Talem autem recursum ad laicos advocatos, et procuratores puniri apud ullam Religionem, nec vidi, nec audivi, ut proinde concludere liceat, ab inolita etiam consuetudine talem recursum in casu, ut praefertur, justificari."

71. *Criminalprocess der Franciscaner,* 243–44; Reiffenstuel, *Jus canoncium,* 5: § VIII, tit. I, num. 519, 64: ". . . appellationem esse manifeste frivolam . . . appellantem ad duplicem poenam condemnare debet." A frivolous appeal was done out of anger or felt injustice, and without further lawful evidence that could exonerate the defendant. For the Theatines and Somaschi, see Chadwick, *Popes,* 240.

72. Allgemeines Verwaltungsarchiv Wien: Bestand Alter Kultus, kath. Kirche 619, Sign. 63, Generalia, 132 ex 1779, fol. 1. The decree that proscribed the Carthusian statute is reprinted in Maass, *Josephinismus,* iii:366.

remained undetected, despite the fact that their constitutions too had been published.[73]

The most severe sentences were prison, galley service (*triremes*), expulsion from the order, and exile (in another province). The prison was defined as a place of confinement without hoods, monastic belts, and tonsure, and thus a place of shame.[74] In a female convent, one could be imprisoned for continuous disregard of any of the vows, including poverty. Incorrigible nuns were to be kept perpetually in prison in order to avoid public offense.[75] The Prioress of the Augustinian convent in Worms, Catharina Antonia Reiderin, reported on 30 September 1778 that in her monastery existed two prisons—one four flights beneath the surface without any daylight, the other six flights above ground. In her monastery, however, nobody was incarcerated or deserved such punishment, she insisted.[76] Galley service as an oarsman was reserved for monks. It was the sentence for a third offense of fornication, sacrilege, or for physical assault of the provincial (*percutio*). Moreover, anyone who hit the General, even if it was just a slap, had to be punished with galley service (*omnino condemnandus est*).[77] This kind of punishment

73. Güntherode, *Römische Religionskasse,* iii:283. If one appealed to anybody (!) outside the regular hierarchy of appeals, one was excommunicated.

74. *Criminalprocess der Franciscaner,* 245; Sinistrari, *Practica criminalis,* 1: tit. V, § IV, 234: "Carceris poena est alicuius reclusio in obserato loco sine chorda, & caputio. Includit privationem actuum legitimorum."

75. Pellizario, *Tractatio de Monialibus,* ch. 8, q. 48, num. 66, 255.

76. Hessisches Staatsarchiv Darmstadt: Bestand E 5 B, Nr. 2334, Prioress Catharina Antonia Reiderin to the General Vicar of Mainz, 30 September 1778, fol. 6.

77. *Criminalprocess der Franciscaner,* 247; Sinistrari, *Practica criminalis,* 1: 1, tit. VI, 333. The German and Bohemian Servites punished an insult to the provincial with four years in prison; see Güntherode, *Römische Religionskasse,* i:281.

spread from Spain, Italy, and France to northern Europe. In secular law it can be found by the 1520s in the Netherlands, and by the 1550s in the Habsburg territories.[78] It is remarkable that anyone who physically harmed the General "had to be condemned," while other offenses, which were trespasses of divine commands, could be exculpated. If a man was condemned to serve on a galley, he was demoted in front of the monastic community. After a speech by the prior, his habit was taken, his head was shaved, he was given secular clothes, and he was handed over to the navy.[79] This demotion also was crucial if the order wanted to hide the fact that the culprit, who was then publicly transported with other criminals to his destination, was a priest. Since his tonsure was shaved off and no habit distinguished him from a layperson, he looked just like any other criminal. Unfortunately, no archival evidence for monks having served as oarsmen has surfaced thus far, but this is likely due to the fact that such cases would have been erased from an order's institutional memory. It is also not specified where such ex-monks would have to serve in the second half of the eighteenth century, since France abandoned galley service in 1748 and the Habsburg lands stopped sentencing convicts to galley service in Venice in 1762, but most likely perpetual imprisonment was the alternative.[80]

78. Langbein, *Torture and the Law of Proof*, 30–31.

79. Sinistrari, *Practica criminalis*, 1: tit. V, num. 108–9, 286–87; cf. *Statuta Generalia Cismontanae (1639)*, ch. 7, num. 13, 55.

80. Langbein, *Torture and the Law of Proof*, 31; Maasburg, *Die Galeerenstrafe*, 14–15; Frauenstädt, "Zur Galeerenstrafe in Deutschland." On galley service in France, see Bamford, *Fighting Ships and Prisons*; Castan and Zysberg, *Histoire des galères*. In the German-speaking lands galley service was already "rare" in 1730, as a judicial dissertation on the sentence in the kingdom of Saxony suggests: Romanus and Brummer, *Dissertatio juridica . . . de perrara poena ad triremes*.

5

Physical Assault and Assassination Attempts in Female Convents

SLAPS OR FISTFIGHTS WERE no minor offenses but were treated as some of the most severe cases that could occur. Hitting a clergyman was punished with excommunication (major ban) outside the cloister and prosecuted inside with no less rigor. The Piarists (1617) are a post-Tridentine order that had regulations similar to those of the Franciscans. For them, even light slaps (*leviter percutere*) were punished with at least one month in prison for the first offense. If one used a piece of wood or a stone to hit a fellow religious and caused a serious wound, the punishment was six months; for other grave wounds, a year.[1] Generally, the more severe the physical harm inflicted upon a religious, the more severe was the punishment. For example, if an attack resulted in mutilation or death, the attacker had to be condemned to

1. *Constitutiones Religionis Clericorum,* p. 2, cap. 9, 346.

galley service.[2] When the archbishop of Mainz investigated the harshness of the Franciscan criminal practice in 1770, the friars stated that their legal texts did not contain any such punishments. They insisted that such regulations were only contained in fifteenth-century statutes, only in use in Spain. This was a lie since the canonical texts were equally binding for the Franciscans of Germany![3] Orders that were involved in healthcare also took precautions in their legal documents to deal with cases in which a member of their order gave medical counsel for an abortion or conducted it, at any stage of the pregnancy. If the fetus died, the religious was charged with homicide.[4] The Camillians punished even the mere possession of weapons with prison.[5]

Less harsh punishments were used for nuns.[6] Not only was every layperson who hit a nun harshly punished by a secular court, but also every nun, but of course by an ecclesiastical court only. The same was also true if she threw a book or stone and hit another sister. Preparing poison to sicken or kill a religious was ranked among the most severe cases, but even more brutal crimes happened. In 1683 in the Norbertine convent of Łęczyca, Poland, Beata Garwanksa

2. *Statuta Generalia Cismontanae*, ch. 7, num. 9, 55.

3. Haus-, Hof-und Staatsarchiv Wien: MEA 72b, 19 February 1770, fol. 33–35; Haus-, Hof-und Staatsarchiv Wien: MEA 72b, 13 February 1770, fol. 57v–58.

4. *Regula et Constitutiones Clericorum regularium*, 92: "Si quis abortum procuraverit, consilium dedderit, aut auxilium ante, vel post animationem foetus, et specialiter effectu secuto." Likewise, Franciscan criminal law mentioned the case of cooperation in an abortion, a crime that deserved death in secular law and lifelong prison or galley service in a monastery (Melfi, *Poenalium*, pt. 1, ch. 4, 157).

5. *Regula et Constitutiones Clericorum regularium ministrantium infirmis* (Rome: 1727), 92.

6. Early modern treatments seem to follow medieval tradition. See Lusset, "Propriae Salutis."

smashed the prioress' head with a bed-warming stone and afterwards smothered the still-breathing nun because she had discovered her secret love for the confessor of the cloister.[7] The only licit way of hitting a nun was in self-defense or for correction, but only if applied by the rightful person. Novices could be hit by any professed sister, while among the nuns only the abbess or her delegate had this privilege. In all other cases, an assaulting nun was excommunicated.[8]

7. Archiwum Państwowe we Wrocławiu/Breslau, Poland: Rep. 67 sygn. 3466b, murder in the Norbertine convent of Łęczyca in 1683. It was a problem for the order to secure the nun because the local convent was not equipped for holding a criminal. Understandably, other monasteries rejected receiving the murderer, Beata Garwanska, as prisoner. Unfortunately, we do not know the fate of this nun. Professor Dr. Ulrich G. Leinsle (Regensburg) brought this case to my attention. A similar murder case is that of Sister Virginia Monza; see Vigorelli, *Vita e processo di suor Virginia Maria de Leyva*.

8. On the punishment of any person hitting a nun, see Pellizario, *Tractatio de Monialibus*, ch. 9, num. 12; for nuns fighting each other, see ch. 8, num 34, 246: ". . . e manibus alterius Monialis . . ." ibid. on poison; on the licit "light" slapping of novices and whether a nun can get the permission of the abbess to slap a professed nun for correction, see ibid., ch. 9, q. 7, num. 13, 262. Pellizario mentions the opinion of Cardinal Cajetan, who supposedly argued that a nun who through surgery or medicine procured an abortion was not (!) excommunicated (ibid., 246). The question whether an abortion of an "inanimate" fetus was better than risking scandal for the monastery was denied by the majority of theologians, since it was considered a grave sin by (different from the above) Cajetan of Alexandris (Alexandris, *Confessarius Monialium*, ch. 11, § 8, q. 3, 449). A theologian who upheld Cardinal Cajetan's position was Monacelli, *Formularium Legale Practicum*, 3:256, because the nun would act in self-defense of her honor (*ad tuendam honorem . . . ad vitandam infamiam*). If it was allowed for a clergyman to kill somebody in self-defense, so it must be for a nun, argued Monacelli (following Thomas Sanchez, SJ [1550–1610] and Jesuit probabilism without mentioning him; on Sanchez, see the groundbreaking study of Alfieri, *Nella camera degli sposi*). For a historical perspective on abortion in Catholic teaching, see Connery, *Abortion*.

A good example of violence and mild punishment in a female convent comes from Oberwerth near Coblenz, Germany. A Benedictine abbey for women of noble birth, which focused on a comfortable lifestyle, the monastery always had problems maintaining monastic discipline. During the last quarter of the eighteenth century, Abbess Maria Leopoldina Aloysia von Boineburg (r. 1773–1791) tried to restore the rule of St. Benedict. Initially, Francisca von Wangen (1764–1813)[9] seemed like a good candidate for monastic life when she applied for the novitiate. In 1784 she expressed her conviction that she was called to religious life in front of diocesan commissioners who oversaw the application process.[10] After her vows, the situation changed dramatically. Von Wangen became depressed and unhappy, especially because of the abbess' rigor. At some point before 1791, in February—the year is unknown—von Wangen was so desperate that she attempted to poison the abbess and prioress. The assassination attempt was detected and von Wangen was immediately confined to the prison. The abbess implored Archbishop and Elector Clemens Wenzeslaus of Trier (r. 1768–1803) to transfer the young woman to another monastic house, and recommended the monastery in Andernach. These poor Franciscan nuns already had some "lodging guests," she informed the bishop—obviously other criminal nuns.[11] Von Wangen wrote to the archbishop in anguish: "Out of the miserable prison, where I sigh since

9. Jeanne Françoise Caroline Wangen died on 5 May 1813 in Coblenz (Zivilstandsregister). Letter of the City Archive of Koblenz of 15 December 2011.

10. Landeshauptarchiv Koblenz: Best 1 C, Nr. 19646, Minutes of a hearing of 19 January 1784 in front of the Archdiocesan Commissioners.

11. Landeshauptarchiv Koblenz: Best 1 C, Nr. 19646, undated letter of Abbess von Boineburg to Archbishop Clemens Wenzeslaus of Trier.

the end of February, thus over five months, I implore your limitless mercy and lenience . . . to be pardoned and freed." She acknowledged the severity of her crime, confessed, and hoped that this would contribute to a more merciful handling of her case in order "to shorten the punishment for the youthful heat and imprudence."

> I acknowledge the greatness of my sin . . . and promise . . . to fully and permanently improve myself . . . after my liberation from this painful incarceration . . . I could not believe . . . considering the kindness of your fatherly heart, which the whole world praises . . . that I, who am in the blossom of my life, would have to do penance until the end of my days or even some substantial time in this sorrowful incarceration, since it was not untamed malice [*Bosheit*] of heart but temporary ardor and rashness [*Übereilung*] that was to blame.[12]

Clemens Wenzeslaus freed von Wangen—but at the insistence of the abbess, who feared for her life, he sent the violent nun to Andernach to do penance in a special cell. She was ordered to behave like a poor Franciscan and to follow the rigorous daily prayer schedule of the monastery. Every three months, the prioress of the Andernach monastery was expected to send a report on the improvement of the criminal nun to the archbishop.[13] The story does not end here. Von Wangen was at some point reintegrated into the community at Oberwerth. In 1791 a new abbess, Maria Carolina de Feignies de l'Atre (d. 1802), had taken over after the natural (?) death of abbess Boineburg. By 1798 the entire convent was exiled to Kamp, because French troops had occupied

12. Landeshauptarchiv Koblenz: Best 1 C, Nr. 19646, undated letter of Francisca von Wangen to Archbishop Clemens Wenzeslaus.

13. Landeshauptarchiv Koblenz: Best 1 C, Nr. 19647.

the Oberwerth lodgings. In this complicated situation, the abbess asked the archbishop for permission to dismiss von Wangen from the order. This time, the reasons were her frequent illegal leaves from the cloister and the public scandal she had caused by the delivery of two children, one in 1796 and one in 1799—the latter fathered by a French officer. No dismissal was granted, but when von Wangen left again—highly pregnant—with a man, the nuns decided to reject her reentrance. Previous attempts to transfer her to female convents in Hadamar and Swabia had been unsuccessful. The abbess preferred that von Wangen live a lascivious life in the city of Coblenz than to let her enter the convent again. The Elector agreed this time and ordered that if von Wangen returned, she was to be incarcerated perpetually.[14]

14. Archiv des Bistums Trier: Abt. 63, 32, Nr. 5, Extract of the protocol of the General Vicar of March 1800. The year the archbishop gives in his handwritten note (1801) must be a mistake.

6

Fornication
and Child Abuse

FORNICATION, OR THE BREAKING of the vow of chastity, was
a major offense punished rigorously in all orders until the
end of the monastic penal system.[1] There is no evidence
that any change occurred in the sanctioning of such behavior, so that one could speak, as Robert Muchembled does,
of a continuous "criminalization of the moral sphere." Monastic regulations and canon law dissertations give detailed
descriptions and discussions of what was sanctioned—for
example, when a nun performed or cooperated in an abortion or if two young males masturbated.[2] In the 1690s, a
canonist recommended that a nun who permitted a man to

1. In secular law, fornication was decriminalized in the second
half of the eighteenth century in most German states; see Hull, *Sexuality, State and Civil Society*, 115n35.

2. Cf. Muchembled, *L'Invention de l'homme moderne*, 154–74;
Spierenburg, *Prison Experience*, 17; for such morals of the laity until
1800, see Schmidt, *Sühne oder Sanktion?*.

have intercourse with her be perpetually incarcerated.[3] A Servite monk who seduced a nun was not only excommunicated but also punished with lifelong captivity.[4] Among the Carmelites, all carnal vices were considered equally offensive. Only for sodomy was a special rule invoked.[5] The Franciscans distinguished between smaller and graver sins against chastity. For a first offense one was "only" sentenced to six months in prison.[6] Sodomitical monks should be handed over to the secular arm for punishment, argued the Franciscan canonist Santoro de Melfi in 1649.[7] In most cases this meant the death penalty—in some areas by fire.[8]

3. Pellizario, *Tractatio de Monialibus*, ch. 4, q. 3, num. 78, 89.

4. Güntherode, *Römische Religionskasse*, iii:282.

5. See also Antonius a Spiritu Sancto, *Directorium Regularium*, tract. 4, disp. 3, § 5, num. 499, 80: "Adverte tamen peccatum carnis intelligi, in hoc statuto omnes species huius peccati excepta sodomia, de quae est specialis lex, nam cum lex non distinguat, nec nos destinguere (!) debemus, & in poenis mitior amplectenda est interpretatio: Unde sub haec lege comprehenditur, non solum fornicatio, adulterium, sacrilegium, raptus, incestus, sed pollutio sive secum, sive altera vel altero, ut bene advertit . . .

6. Most regularly quoted by seventeenth- and eighteenth-century canonists is Santoro de Melfi (or Santorus a Melphio), *Poenalium Districtionum Examen*, pt. 1, ch. 8 (de poenis in castitatis violatores sancitis [!]), 345–84. Santoro distinguishes between simple fornication, "mollities" (effeminacy: "Mollities enim est contra naturam, quia extra usum naturae provocatur semen, omne autem peccatum . . ."), bestiality, incest, "stuprum" (defloration of a virgin), and adultery (ibid., 352). The first two were the least offensive, while the others were considered egregious offenses. Cf. Melfi, *Compendium*, 102, also mentions the crime of alchemy, which was punished according to the will of the provincial; ibid., 108, gambling is mentioned as a crime.

7. Melfi, *Poenalium*, pt. 1, ch. 8, 376.

8. See, for example, the case of Georg Gunzenhäuser in 1626 (Stadtarchiv Stuttgart: Bestand 914, Nr. 328), who was sentenced to death by fire by the secular court of Ulm. This punishment was altered to decapitation followed by the burning of the corpse. For homosexuality in the early modern era the literature is vast, but a

If one did not hand over a person guilty of the "unnamable vice" (*innominabili scelere*), which was usually sodomy, then this monk was first stripped of his clothes and flagellated in the harshest possible way by the entire community. Afterwards he was perpetually detained in the dishonorable prison.[9] Thus far I am aware of only one religious order, the

good overview is given by Puff, "Early Modern Europe, 1400–1700," and for Germany in particular Puff, *Sodomy in Reformation Germany and Switzerland*. An important study on the administrative control of sexuality and its penal history in early modern France is Taeger, *Intime Machtverhältnisse*. Taeger refutes Foucault's claim in his *Histoire de la sexualité* (1978) that in eighteenth-century France a broad interest in condoning non-heterosexual, non-monogamous relationships existed and especially the role of the *philosophes* in this alleged sexual emancipation. Her résumé is: "Die Aufklärung mag der revolutionären Gesetzgebung den Weg bereiten, im Hinblick auf die strafrechtliche Würdigung der Sodomie aber ist ihr Einfluss ebensowenig revolutionierend, wie die permissive Haltung der revolutionären Gesetzgeber angesichts dieser Materie eine wirklich originelle. Nicht die öffentliche Kritik–sondern verunsicherte absolute Monarchen, nicht das revolutionäre Freiheitsversprechen–sondern die politische Klugheit sich etablierender Polizeichefs wirken in Frankreich auf eine Erweiterung individueller Gestaltunsgmöglichkeiten von Intimität hin." Cf. also Spetor, Puff, and Herzog, *After the History of Sexuality*.

9. Sinistrari, *Practica criminalis,* 1: tit. VI, § 38, 334: "Qui de innominabili scelere confessus, vel convictus fuerit, nudus cum soli femoralibus, in coetu Fratrorum, ligatis manibus, ac recitans Psalmum: Miserere mei Deus, durissimi flagellari, ac leviusculis flammis hinc inde circumpositis quodammodo comburi & ad perpetuos carceres irrevocabiliter damnari debet, ubi in pane & aqua tribus saltem in hebdomada diebus jejunet. Si autem in idem scelsus relapsus fuerit, ad triremes perpetuo destinari." It is unclear to me how one can relapse into homosexuality in solitary confinement.

Also, the Order of the Discalced Mercedarians had a similar harsh punishment for homosexual acts (under the chapter heading "De incorrigibilibus"), see *Constitutiones Sacri et Regalis Ordinis PP. Excalceatorum B. Mariae Virginae de Mercede,* ch. 33, 141: "Si aliquis in peccatum indicibile (quod Deus avertat) lapsus fuerit, propter huiusmodi criminis gravitatem, & foeditatem, & quia maxime nocivum est communitati, de eoque raro emendatio praesumitur, decernimus,

Hieronymites of the Congregation of Peter of Pisa (*Ordo Fratrum Eremitarum S. Hieronymi, Congregationis B. Petri de Pisis*), which after sentencing a sodomitical monk to life-long imprisonment allowed the possibility of release after ten years if the General Chapter of the order agreed.[10]

It must be noted that in the early modern era "sod-omy" could be a variety of things, but sodomy *proper* was understood in canon law according to Pius V's bull *Hor-rendum illud scelus* (1568), and in monastic constitutions as *concubitus maris cum masculo per vas praeposterum*, that is, anal intercourse between two males. This is important because only this act was punished with the utmost sever-ity—normally the extradition of the convict to the secular

---

ut qui de hoc peccato convictus fuerit, ab Ordine expellatur. . . . Si vero aliquis vehementer fuerit suspectus, carceri perpetuo tradatur: nisi alias per diffinitorium generale cum eo benigne fuerit dispen-satum. Denique, quoties quis aliquod delictum gravius, & atrotius perpetraverit, in Patris Vicarii Generalis, vel Provincialis, & duorum Diffinorum, aut Praelatorum arbitrio sit judicare, an ab Ordine expeli debeat." Cf. also the constitutions of the Carmelites, *Constitutiones Fratrum (1736)*, ch. 6, num. 4, 354. Barbosa, *Summa Apostolicarum decisionum,* collect. 130, 137 quotes the constitution *Omnipotentes* of 20 March 1623 of Pope Gregory XV: "Carceribus perpetuis seu muro clauditur, qui sortilegiis pactum fecerit cum diabolo, & a fide apostataverit, si infirmitas, divortia, aut impotentia generandi secuta fuerit, sive animalibus, fruibus, aut fructibus damnum dederit: sed si mors est secuta, traditur Curiae seculari." Likewise the constitutions of the Cistercians prescribed lifelong prison for homosexuality, see Paris, *Nomasticon Cisterciense,* 2nda pars, dist. 7 (De causis ordinis et correctione culparum), cap. 8 (De detractoribus), 533 :"Qui vero pro huiusmodi vitio carceri sunt mancipati, in eodem sint carcere usque ad terminum vitae suae." The punishment for sodomy of young boys was lenient (Passerino, *Regulare Tribunal,* q. 28, num. 27, 402: "In crimine vero sodomiae impubes muliebria passus per vim, & metum, si de hoc constet, nulla poena punitur").

10. Holsten and Brockie, *Codex Regularium Monasticarum,* vi: ch. XI, 99.

authority and punishment by death.[11] Such an extradition, however, would have made the case public and would have harmed the order's reputation. Since I have not come across any records of public executions of sodomitical monastic clergy in eighteenth-century Germany, it is likely that if the secular authorities were not informed by the victim of a rape or an illicit relationship, and thus forced to act, the monastery solved such cases internally.

However, mutual masturbation with another male (*pollutio cum altero*), or with a woman, an animal, or a demon, was subsumed under the label *peccatum nefandum*, but did not deserve the greatest harshness of the law, according to the Portuguese Carmelite Antonius a Spiritu Sancto. If, however, one committed such an offense, one should—in Portugal—be handed over to the Inquisition.[12] Despite such strict directives, there is evidence that suggests that especially when children were involved, the law was not always executed. In a 1653 case from Speyer, Germany, it seems that an eleven-year-old boy who appeared to have suffered shock after being raped by the Augustinian prior was not believed, but instead the prior argued that through negligence the child had suffered a bad chill and consequently a mental disturbance.[13] If a monk entrusted with the care of a female prisoner had intercourse with her, he deserved lifelong imprisonment or galley service. The deed was considered even more despicable if he used force (*cum violentia*), that is, raped her.[14]

11. Pius V, "Horrendum Illud Scelus (30 August, 1568)," in *Magnum Bullarium Romanum,* ii: 287.

12. Antonius a Spiritu Sancto, *Directorium Regularium,* tract. III, disp. 4, sect. 6, num. 69, num. 74, 148

13. Stadtarchiv Speyer: 1 A404. Unfortunately, it is not known how the case ends, but since the file contains nothing about a conviction, it seems that the accusation was not believed and that church authorities did not sentence the prior.

14. Melfi, *Poenalium,* pt. 1, ch. 4, 157.

A well-documented case of fornication is that of a monk in Prüm, near Trier, Germany, in 1769. An undated and anonymous letter of one of the monks of the Benedictine abbey denounced the disharmonious situation there. The new prior—Prüm did not have an abbot but was subject to the bishop of Trier—was using, according to the complaint, physical force to punish the vices of his fellow monks. Instead of correcting with love, he was yelling at the monks or literally pushing them around. However, another monk was the real villain. On 6 March 1769, the seniors of the abbey gathered to interrogate P. Johannes Figulus, who had been subprior for eighteen years, on the basis of a denunciation that he was a pedophile. The first question was who his confessor was and whether he had been honest in the confessional, which he affirmed. The prior conducted the trial according to the canon law handbooks of the Jesuit Franz Schmalzgrueber (1663–1735). The files only survived in the archives because the archbishop was in charge of this monastery. The trial records show that there was no fear of recording the disgustingly detailed descriptions of the crime. For example, Figulus was asked if his previous prior had forbidden him to take "the small children with him to bed in his cell and . . . to commit blasphemies with them." He affirmed this as well, and confessed that he had seduced children—only altar boys—by bribing them with bread. The previous prior had admonished him not only once, but several times, to stop this behavior. His abuse was not singular, but happened two to three times a week, and in 1768 alone he had molested five different boys.[15] When in 1770 he fell

15. Figulus denied, however, having had sexual intercourse with adult men. The questions became more detailed, for example: "Whether it is true that he had once or more often touched the penis [*membrum virile*] of small boys of 12, 13 or 14 years of age," which he affirmed. Likewise he affirmed that he often "put off his clothes in his cell in presence of a boy and presented this innocent child his

back into his old behavior and on 20 August abused two
ten-year-old boys after compline, harsher measures than
admonitions were necessary.[16] Again Figulus confessed and
promised to do everything to mend his ways and asked for
clemency.[17] This time, however, the recently inaugurated
Archbishop Clemens Wenzeslaus decreed his perpetual
detainment.[18] This case demonstrates that even for the
peccatum sodomisticum or pedophilia, eighteenth-century
monastic communities were not always willing to actually
enforce strict canon law. Instead, the former subprior was
admonished over and over again, and thus given the chance
to molest even more children. Only when the crime was

---

proprium membrum virile to touch it." These sexual meetings occurred usually after he had said Mass. It seems he let the boys urinate
in front of him, made them drunk, asked them to masturbate and let
"the pollution run in his hands." Afterwards he massaged the sperm
on his whole body, and did the same with the sperm of the child. He
also confessed to have persuaded the boys to eat the sperm "since
it tasted sweet like meadow salsify [*bocksbardt*]." He tore down the
pants of another boy and attempted to rape him but did not complete
the *peccatum sodomisticum*. Already in 1766 he had been admonished by the prior and the entire monastery for his sexual escapades
and was able to abstain from his crimes for a about a year, while in
the last year, 1768, he had committed sodomy several times in the
dormitory or the infirmary, with about five different boys, who are all
named in the protocol. Landeshauptarchiv Koblenz: Best. 18, 2182,
Protocoll of 6 March 1769.

16. Landeshauptarchiv Koblenz: Best. 18, 2182. Letter of 7 September 1770. Now he had the boys also flagellate themselves and
abused them for oral and anal sex. Landeshauptarchiv Koblenz: Best.
18, 2182. Letter of the diocesan commissioner Heinrich Joseph Berg
to Archbishop Clemens Wenzeslaus of 29 September 1770.

17. Figulus had been ordained in 1738. If one assumes a regular
age of twenty-five at the time of ordination, then Figulus would have
been about fifty-six in 1770. (Letter from the Archives of the Diocese
of Trier, 17 February 2009).

18. Archiv des Bistums Trier: Abt. 63.7, Nr. 8, Decree of Clemens
Wenzeslaus, 29 October 1770.

revealed to the state authority, in this case the archbishop of
Trier, were measures taken to protect the young and to punish the delinquent. Unlike state proceedings, nothing in this
case suggests concern about homosexuality as a "biological
depletion" and the seduction of children as the ruin of po-
tentially sexually potent fathers and rationally calculating
members of society.[19]

19. Cf. Hull, *Sexuality, State and Civil Society*, 148.

7

Escapes from the Cloister

PROFESSED NUNS WHO LEFT the cloister illicitly committed a grave sin, which could be punished with excommunication (*majoris latae sententiae Papae reservate*).[1] Again, the noble Benedictine abbey of Oberwerth near Koblenz provides an example. Since the abbess had tightened discipline in 1780, a nun, Lucretia von Münster, had decided to leave the cloister without any dispensation. She had taken off to Würzburg for "medical reasons" to stay with her mother. "Nothing consoles me more," wrote the abbess of Oberwerth, "than the fact that this girl is at least constantly under the watch of her mother and then . . . in the female monastery of St. Afra in Würzburg, which belongs to our

---

1. Pellizario, *Tractatio de Monialibus*, ch. 5, q. 10, num. 17, 113. On the often lenient punishment in the Middle Ages—in order to avoid scandal—see Fossier, "Propter vitandum scandalum"; Vannotti, "Monasterium exivit."

order."[2] Abbess and archbishop called her back.[3] Despite her illicit absence, she was not imprisoned, which shows that the laws were leniently applied. In early August 1783, the unhappy nun approached the archbishop of Trier with an official request for a dispensation from her vows. For ten years she had suffered in the monastery, had bad health, and could hardly sustain the fasting, she claimed. She tried to convince him that she did not want to leave because of her alleged "desire for freedom" but because she wanted to live in "tranquility and contentment," and this would not be possible in Oberwerth but only with her parents in Würzburg.[4] Archbishop Clemens Wenzeslaus forwarded her request and supported it, and obviously believed that she was incapable of complying with monastic duties and that she had taken the vows while she was mentally disturbed (*perturbantia mentis*). Should she stay, he argued, it would

2. Landeshauptarchiv Koblenz: Best 1 C, Nr. 19646, Letter of Abbess von Boineburg of 23 January 1780 to Archbishop Clemens Wenzeslaus of Trier. The often repeated claim that Boineburg was the last abbess is incorrect. The last abbess was Maria Carolina de Feignies de l'Atre. On her death in 1802, see Archiv des Bistums Trier: Abt. 63, 32, Nr. 6 regarding her burial and estate. Cf. also Stromberg, *Denkwürdiger und nützlicher Antiquarius*, 2/1:248–49. In 1791 the convent had eleven members, including abbess and prioress. In 1794 the building was evacuated and the convent relocated to Kamp.

3. Landeshauptarchiv Koblenz: Best 1 C, Nr. 19646, Letter of Archbishop Clemens Wenzeslaus to the Abbess of Oberwerth of 25 January 1780.

4. Landeshauptarchiv Koblenz: Best 1 C, Nr. 19646, Letter of Lucretia von Münster, undated. Another Lucretia von Münster had an almost two-decades-long romantic relationship with Adam Friedrich von Seinsheim (1708–1779) before his ordination to the priesthood (Renner, "Jugend- und Studienzeit der Brüder Adam Friedrich und Josef Franz von Seinsheim," 262–67). One is reminded of the Tencin siblings (Pierre and Claudine-Alexandrine), who in Paris fought in the 1720s for the annulment of their vows (McManners, *Church and Society*, 2:416).

lead to the inevitable demise of her soul (*vota . . . imprudenter emissa inevitablis ruina*). Von Münster, however, became impatient and on 5 September 1783 pestered a high-ranking official of the bishop—obviously she had not been told that her case had already been forwarded to Rome. She indirectly threatened the authorities with suicide and described the fantasy she had when the doctor let her bleed: "so that when I was drained of blood I intended to loosen the band [*Bindewinde*] and to bleed to death." Suicide was considered a mortal sin that condemned one to hell, and even the attempt was punishable; moreover, a superior had to do everything to prevent such an act, and naturally the most secure way was to lock up such a person. But again, nothing happened.[5] On 19 September 1783, the Sacred Congregation for Religious and the pope approved her wish. Her family was informed that she was dispensed and could live for the rest of her days with them but could not marry.[6] The case of Lucretia von Münster, despite her

5. Landeshauptarchiv Koblenz: Best 1 C, Nr. 19646, Letter of Lucretia von Münster to an unnamed Geheimrat of 5 September 1783, num. 14: "Should you have forgotten a case of such importance? No—I cannot believe that because it does not only pertain to my miserable life, which is my fate for ten years and the source of a chain of pains and sorrows, but also my soul, which would get lost if I had to die here . . . pain and persecution increase daily . . . so that when I was drained of blood I intended to loosen the band [*Bindewinde*] and to bleed to death . . . only the thought of it terrified me so much that I fainted and could not move at all for two hours . . . The most loving providence has liberated me from suicide [*Selbstmorde*]."

6. Her family was not so happy about the dispensation. One of her siblings (due to the unreadable signature, it is unclear whether the letter was written by one of her sisters of her brothers) was utterly surprised to hear that the monastic context would cause physical health problems for Lucretia von Münster: "What your Excellency writes about the vocation of my sister I am . . . in complete agreement, however my sister was no child when she asked to enter the religious state. My family and I have admonished her . . . to reason carefully

illicit trip and her openly confessed suicide fantasies, shows that harsh punishments were not inflicted in every case of a fugitive religious. Perhaps, however, this was an exception since the religious was of noble birth.

It seems that men were more likely to be imprisoned, and often the fear of imprisonment motivated an escape, which made one "infamous" and deprived one of all rights in the monastic community. In Memmingen, the Augustinian Conrad Mayer escaped on 16 September 1766 because he had been incarcerated the previous day for contradicting the superior concerning the infallibility of the pope. He feared more than just a simple overnight imprisonment would await him. At night he climbed out of his window on the second floor and escaped to the free imperial and Protestant city of Memmingen, from whose magistrate he requested religious asylum. Since the city was surrounded by Catholic territories, the magistrates had to plan a secret route on which the ex-monk could travel without having to fear extradition. On the way, a Catholic mob stopped the cart, arrested the monk, and brought him back to his monastery. Protests that the right of religious asylum had been broken were rejected because Mayer had not officially converted, but was just a disobedient monk. Mayer remained in the Lauingen monastery in prison for the next twenty years. He reappeared in March 1785 when a fistfight between two drunken Augustinians broke out in an inn in Memmingen. One of them was Conrad Mayer. A friar had attempted to transport him

---

and to feel inside her [*sich wohl vorher zu bedenken und sich genau zu fühlen*] before . . . she enters . . . religious life. All this was repeated and communicated to her before her profession of vows and she was assured that it would not in the least harm her reputation if she left the monastery before her vows, but that everybody would regard her as a reasonable [*vernünftige*] person . . . and that the family would welcome her again." Landeshauptarchiv Koblenz: Best 1 C, Nr. 19646, Letter of X von Münster of 22 September 1783.

to a different house of the order, yet after they had reached the free territory of Memmingen, Mayer struggled to escape. While the first attempt failed, the second was successful since his guards were already heavily intoxicated from a beer-stop they had taken. This time the city made no mistakes. The asylum seeker was given a letter of recommendation and put on the next sled to Ulm—he fell off twice because he was so drunk—and arrived safely the next morning, where he began his new life as a Protestant.[7] A similarly fascinating account of an escape story is given in the autobiography of the former Augustinian Joseph Spenn, who after his religious life became a medical doctor.[8]

Like nuns, monks who left the cloister without permission were punished in principle, depending on the circumstances of their absences. For example, if a religious decided to use an official business trip for a grand tour but remained faithful to his vows, in contact with the abbot, and returned, he could get away with a mild punishment or none at all.[9] Monks or nuns who were suspected of attempts to escape for good were interned, and if they had escaped several times and were recaptured, it was most common to imprison them for life. One monk, the Cistercian Innocent Morazi of Waldsassen, Germany, in the Upper Palatinate,[10]

7. Petz, *Letzte Hexe*, 120–23; 172–73. Cf. Stadtarchiv Memmingen: A 367/01 and Hauptstaatsarchiv Stuttgart: Prämonstratenserkloster Rot an der Rot, B 487 Bü 10.

8. Spenn, *Lebensbeschreibung Joseph Spenns*.

9. See Lehner, *Enlightened Monks*, 47–52.

10. Binhack, "Geschichte des Cistercienser-Stiftes Waldsassen," 266–70; Binhack, "Drei Jahre aus der Geschichte der Abtei Waldsassen, 1792–1795," 262–64. A warrant of apprehension and warning about Morazi was printed in *Staats-Relation der neuesten europäischen Nachrichten*, 35. Wochenstück (3 September 1784), 39. For documentation of some of his escapes, see Bayerisches Hauptstaatsarchiv München: Bayerische Zisterzienserkongregation Nr. 29.

escaped eighteen times successfully, including from imprisonment in manacles. Another, the Carthusian Athanasius König (b. 1665) of Aggsbach, escaped four times between 1692 and 1699.[11]

Religious orders often hired bounty hunters to get such individuals back into the cloister, and even circulated warrants such as that for the Dominican Martin Engelhardt of 1702, who was wanted for escaping the cloister, adultery, theft, and lèse-majesté.[12] Such cases were certainly exceptional, but in the eighteenth century the number of unhappy monks was increasing rapidly. Superiors had to deal for the first time since the Reformation with greater numbers of openly discontented religious.[13] Nevertheless, almost no descriptions of the trials that condemned such monks and nuns exist. An exception is the case of the Augustinian canon and well-known composer Benedict Geisler (1696–1772) of Triefenstein, near Würzburg, Germany, but again the records survived only because the diocese was involved.

Geisler had entered the canonry of Triefenstein in 1720 and published his first composition in 1738. In 1727, just three years after his priestly ordination, he escaped and lived for two years in France.[14] He returned and was reconciled with the community. The second time he ran

11. He was incarcerated three times and after the fourth escape expelled from the order, after which nobody attempted to bring him back. Aigner, "Überlegungen zu Herkunft, Leben und sozialer Vernetzung der Aggsbacher Kartäuser," 22, 25.

12. Haus-, Hof- und Staatsarchiv Wien: MEA K 20.

13. On the escapes of the Erfurt Carthusian Nikolaus Listermann (d. 1786), see Mangei, "Klosterhaft und Klosterregel," 61; Simmert, *Die Geschichte der Kartause zu Mainz*, 63–64.

14. Staatsarchiv Würzburg: Geistliche Sachen 302/32, Propst Augustinus to the Bishop of Würzburg of 22 May 1748. For the biographical data of Geisler, see Walter, "Benedikt Geisler. Ein fränkischer Klosterkomponist," 168–93.

away, in 1745, he lived for two years around Nuremberg and Fürth and most likely became Protestant. Due to warrants of apprehension his whereabouts became known and he was incarcerated—albeit very mildly, despite his severe crime of apostasy—in the "honorable prison." He received regular food and drink, but on 18 March 1748, he escaped for the third time: "Nobody can conceive how he could have broken up the door" the prior wrote to the bishop of Würzburg. In Lohr he was identified, disguised as a beggar, and was detained two days afterwards. When he was questioned about why he had escaped he said he desired to go to Rome and ask personally for papal dispensation from his vows, but the documents found in his backpack proved otherwise. He had forged credentials and invented the identity of a Fidelis Sander of the Third Order of St. Francis, which would have ensured his safe travel to Protestant lands.[15] The bishop of Würzburg's delegate, canon Franz Christoph von Zobel von Giebelstadt (1719–1763), and Otto Philipp Erhard Ernst Gross von und in Trockau, canon in Bamberg, approved his imprisonment but asked that the gifted man be given spiritual counsel for the rest of lifelong imprisonment.[16] The Ecclesiastical Council of Würzburg had stated on 24 March 1748 in an official decree

15. Staatsarchiv Würzburg: Geistliche Sachen 302/32, Propst Augustinus to the Bishop of Würzburg of 22 May 1748: "he had also stolen three silver spoons from our convent . . . and other things he needed for his journey. In the letter of recommendation he forged he assumed the identity of the Prior of the Capuchins in Cologne, and declared that he was a friar who had been captivated in the Dutch War some years ago, was robbed of his habit and had to live as a beggar . . . in order to collect the money to buy a new habit. *Sed omnia sunt falsa*. He now sits . . . in a secure place from which he cannot possibly escape and will have to do his penitential exercises . . ."

16. Staatsarchiv Würzburg: Geistliche Sachen 302/32. On Zobel, see Wendehorst, *Benediktinerabtei und das adelige Säkularkanonikerstift St. Burkard in Würzburg*, 249.

to the abbot of Triefenstein that Geisler should be regarded as incorrigible and kept in a prison from which he could not escape.[17] According to the statutes of the Augustinian canons, the abbot began a trial that ended in June 1748. Together with a diocesan commissioner he interrogated Geisler, who according to the statutes of the order was considered incorrigible and sentenced to life in prison.[18] The abbot made sure that he could never be released by a well-meaning person and asked the advice of many erudite canonists, who obviously recommended that Geisler accept his fate. And indeed, the abbot "made out of the necessity a virtue, and persuaded him to endure the purgatory of this world so that he could save his soul."[19] After twenty-four years of solitary imprisonment, Geisler died in 1772.

17. Staatsarchiv Würzburg: Geistliche Sachen 302/32, decree of the Ecclesiastical Council of 24 March 1748.

18. Staatsarchiv Würzburg: Geistliche Sachen 302/32, Propst Augustinus to the Bishop of Würzburg of 10 June 1748: "Si quis omnino incorrigibilis fuerit, et saepe correptus emendare se noluerit, aut sine gravi scandalo totius conventus tolerari non possit, talis, ne contagione pestifera alios perdat, perpetuo incarceretur." Unknown to the abbot was that Eusebius Amort, *Vetus Disciplina Canonicorum Regularium & Saecularium*, 2:624 demonstrated that this rule was used in all established Augustinian canonries.

19. Staatsarchiv Würzburg: Geistliche Sachen 302/32, Propst Augustinus to the Bishop of Würzburg of 10 June 1748.

Conclusion

MONASTERY PRISONS WERE NOT invented by anti-religious Enlightenment writers but were a reality of monastic life. Little differentiated them from medieval dungeons until the eighteenth century, when severe pressure from state authorities, who no longer accepted practices rivaling personal jurisdiction, put an official end to such prisons. In many monasteries, however, dungeons continued to exist until harsher government laws threatened orders with dissolution if they did not comply.

Monastic criminal law prescribed torture and physical punishment and left religious in many orders, especially among the mendicants, vulnerable to the authority of their superiors, who could deny appeals to higher courts or imprison them if the right pretext were found (or simply invented). Monastic regulations forbade revealing any information about internal problems to the public, especially regarding "criminal" offenses; documents pertaining to these cases were regularly destroyed, and government authorities, as well as the public, were misled. If one wanted to use the term, one could certainly speak of a "cover-up" of crimes committed by the clergy in order to avoid public scandal, and this medieval policy continued throughout early modernity and well into the twentieth century.[1] Due to a policy of secrecy regarding clergy crimes, a reevaluation of early modern religious discipline seems to be necessary. To my knowledge, historians have not taken this "cover-up" seriously enough when assessing historical accounts of the achievements of the Tridentine reforms of clergy and religious life. Can sources that claim the high moral standing and improvement of the clergy after Trent be trusted if evidence to the contrary was intentionally destroyed? I think we still can and should trust these post-Tridentine sources, due to their vast number. This study on crime and punishment does not therefore question the positive turnaround in the morals of early modern clergymen and monastics after the Council of Trent, but rather insists that for a complete picture of such a renewal one also has to take into consideration the moral failings of, and crimes committed by, monks and nuns.

1. Cf. Fossier, "Propter vitancum scandalum."

Bibliography

ARCHIVAL SOURCES

Austria

Haus-, Hof-und Staatsarchiv Wien
  MEA 72b
  MEA K 20
Allgemeines Verwaltungsarchiv Wien
  Bestand Alter Kultus, kath. Kirche 619, Sign. 63

Germany

Bischöfliches Zentralarchiv Regensburg
  Kartause Prüll, KL 31a Nr. 8
Bayerisches Hauptstaatsarchiv München
  · Bayerische Benediktinerkongregation, Rubrik 48
  Benediktbeuern, Nr. 6.
  Kurbaiern Geistlicher Rat, Aufsicht über die Klöster, vorl. Sign.
  Schaeftlarn 24
  Bayerische Zisterzienserkongregation Nr. 29.
Stadtarchiv Speyer
  1 A404.
Diözesanarchiv Rottenburg
  A I 2 c, Nr. 144, 145 and 146

Bibliography

Stadtarchiv Stuttgart
    Bestand 914, Nr. 328
Hessisches Staatsarchiv Darmstadt
    Bestand E 5 B, Nr. 2334,
Hauptstaatsarchiv Stuttgart
    B 40 Bü 478
    B 38 I Bü 1144 und 1445
    Prämonstratenserkloster Rot an der Rot, B 487 Bü 10.
Stadtarchiv Memmingen
    A 367/01
Staatsarchiv Würzburg
    Geistliche Sachen 302/32
Archiv des Bistums Trier
    Abt. 63.7, Nr. 8
    Abt. 63, 32, Nr. 5
Landeshauptarchiv Koblenz
    Best. 18, 2182
    Best. 1 C, Nr. 19646
    Best 1 C, Nr. 19647
Staatsarchiv Würzburg
    HV Ms. f. 205
Landesarchiv Nordrhein-Westfalen-Hauptstaatsarchiv Düsseldorf
    Kurköln VIII, 795

Poland

Archiwum Państwowe we Wrocławiu/Breslau, Poland
    Rep. 67 sygn. 3466b

PRIMARY SOURCES

Alexandris, Cajetan de. *Confessarius Monialium commoda, brevi & practica methodo instructus.* Cologne: 1728.
Amort, Eusebius. *Vetus Disciplina Canonicorum Regularium et Saecularium.* Vol. 2. Venice: 1747.
Annales Ordinis Cartusienis. Vol. 1. Correriae: 1687.
Anonymous. "Beleuchtung der vorgeblichen Bestättigung der Geschichte des Pater Anians im Journal von und für Franken."

Kritik über gewisse Kritiker, Rezensenten, und Broschürenmacher 6 (1792) 209–22.

———. "Gesinnungen eines österreichischen Mönches nach der Aufhebung seines Klosters." *Der deutsche Zuschauer,* edited by Peter Adolph Winkopp, 1 (1785) 263–78.

———. *Magdalena Paumann oder die eingekerkerte Nonne im Angerkloster zu München.* Munich: 1870.

———. "Neuester Versuch, die Inquisition im Neapolitanischen einzuführen." *Le Bret's Magazin zum Gebrauch der Staaten- und Kirchengeschichte* 3 (1773) 160–95.

———. "Trauriges Schicksal des P. Anianus, weiland gewesenen Lectors der Philosophie und Theologie im Capucinerkloster zu Bamberg." *Journal von und für Franken* 2 (1791) 177–84.

———. "Widerlegung der Fabel von P. Anian." *Kritik über gewisse Kritiker, Rezensenten und Broschürenmacher* 5 (1791) 267–72.

Antonius a Spiritu Sancto. *Directorium Regularium. Pars prima, quae est de privilegiis regularium.* Lyon: 1661.

Barbosa, Augustinus. *Summa Apostolicarum decisionum extra jus commune vagantium.* Lyon: 1645.

Becker, Ferdinand. *Geschichte meiner Gefangenschaft im Franziskanerkloster zu Paderborn: Ein Beitrag zur Sitten- und Aufklärungsgeschichte des Hochstifts Paderborn.* Rudolstadt: 1799.

Born, Ignaz von. *Monachologie nach linnäischer Methode.* Frankfurt: 1802.

Calmet, Augustin. *Commentarius litteralis historico-moralis in regulam S.P. Benedicti.* Vol. 1. Linz: 1750.

Codex Redactus Legum Fratrum Minorum in synopsim cum indice copioso. Rome: 1796.

Constitutiones et Extravagantes Ordinis Monachorum S. Hieronymi. Rome: 1730.

Constitutiones Fratrum Coelestinorum Proviniciae Franco-Gallicanae. Paris: 1670.

Constitutiones Fratrum Discalceatorum Beatis Virginis Mariae de Monte Carmelo Congregationis Hispaniae (1736). Madrid: 1737.

Constitutiones Fratrum Discalceatorum Beatissimae Virginis Mariae de Monte Carmelo Primitivae Observantiae Congregationis Hispaniae. Madrid: 1787.

Constitutiones Religionis Clericorum Regularium Pauperum Matris Dei Scholarum Piarum. Rome: 1782.

Constitutiones Sacri et Regalis Ordinis PP. Excalceatorum B. Mariae Virginae de Mercede, Redemptionis Captivorum. Madrid: 1755.

Constitutiones Societatis Jesu Anno 1558. London: 1838.

Bibliography

Constitutiones Urbanae Ordinis Fratrum Minorum S. Francisci
Conventualium. Venice: 1757.

Der Criminalprocess der Franciscaner. Strasburg: 1769.

Eisenschmid, Leonhard Martin. Römisches Bullarium, oder Auszüge
der merkwürdigsten päpstlichen Bullen: aus authentischen
Quellen, durch alle Jahrhundert bis auf die neueste Zeit. 2 vols.
Neustadt: 1831.

Fagnani, Prospero. Commentaria in secundam partem quinti libri.
Rome: 1661.

Fessler, Ignaz Aurelius. Rückblicke auf seine siebzigjaehrige
Pilgerschaft. Breslau: 1824.

Geismar, Martin von. Die politische Literatur der Deutschen im 18.
Jahrhundert. Vol. 2. Leipzig: 1819.

Güntherode, Karl von. Das römische Gesetzbuch. N.p., 1787.

———. Die römische Religionskasse: ein Anhang zum Römischen
Gesetzbuch, oder die in Teutschland noch zu wenig bekannten
Grundsätze des römischen Hofes aus Päpstlichen Bullen gezogen.
3 vols. Karlsruhe: 1787–88.

Habsheim, Bonagratia von. Summula selectarum questionum
regularium quas in specialem usum FF. Capucinorum. Cologne:
1667.

Hasse, Johann Friedrich [Linus]. Klosterzwang und Klosterflucht,
oder Leben und Begebenheiten des gewesenen Kapuziner-Mönchs
Johann Friedrich Hasse. Germany: 1805.

Held, Willebold. Jurisprudentia universalis ex juribus canonico,
civilo Romano, et Germanico . . . Liber V: De judiciis causarum
criminalium. Memmingen: 1773.

Holsten, Lukas, and Marianus Brockie, eds. Codex Regularum
Monasticarum et Canonicarum. 6 vols. Augsburg: 1758–59.

Howard, John. The State of the Prisons in England and Wales.
Warrington: 1777.

Katzenberger, Kilian. Liber Vitae seu compendiosa expositio litteralis
in Sacram Regulam S. P. Francisci Seraphici. Augsburg: 1761.

Kerckhove, Gaudentius van der. Methodus corrigendi Regulares.
Bruges: 1701.

Kutschenpeitscher, Ignaz Loyola [also known as Ignaz von Born].
Neueste Naturgeschichte des Mönchthums. N.p., 1783. 1802
reprint published under the title Monachologie. Frankfurt and
Leipzig: 1802.

Lipowsky, Felix Joseph. Gemälde aus dem Nonnenleben. Munich:
1808.

Mabillon, Jean. "Réflexions sur les prisons des orders religieux." In
    Ouvrages Posthumes, 2:321–35. Paris: F. Babuty et al., 1724.
Magnum Bullarium Romanum a Beato Leone Magno usque ad S.N.D.
    Benedictum XIV. Edited by Laertius Cherubini. Vols. 2–3.
    Luxemburg: 1742.
Magnum Bullarium Romanum seu eiusdem continuatio: Complectens
    Constitutiones a Clemente X & Innocentio XI. Vol. 11.
    Luxemburg: 1739.
Melfi, Santoro da [Santorus a Melphio]. *Compendium in libros*
    poenalium atque Commentariorum super statua generalia totius
    Ordinis seraphici. Rome: 1686.
————. *Poenalium Districtionum Examen, quibus regulares*
    punitivam justitiam administrant. Rome: 1649.
Monacelli, Francisco. *Formularium Legale Practicum Fori*
    Ecclesiastici. Vol. 3. Venice: 1751.
Oehninger, Mansueto. *Wölfe in Schaf-Kleidern.* Leipzig: 1775.
Paris, Julianus. *Nomasticon Cisterciense seu antiquiores Ordinis*
    Ciserciensis constitutions. Paris: 1664.
Passerino, Petro Maria. *Regulare Tribunal seu Praxis Formandi*
    Processus nedum in foro Regularium sed etiam Secularium.
    Rome: 1677.
Pellizario, Francisco. *Tractatio de Monialibus [1646].* Rome: 1755.
Pilati, Leopold. *Origines juris pontificii ad Carolum Sextum.* Trent:
    1739.
Pirhing, Ernricus. *Jus canonicum in V libros Decretalium distributum*
    [1677]. Vol. 5. Dillingen: 1722.
Pius V. *Horrendum illud scelus.* In *Magnum Bullarium Romanum,*
    a Beato Leone Magne usque ad S.D.N. Benedictum XIV: Editio
    Novissima, edited by Laertius Cherubini, 2:287. Luxemburg:
    1752.
Regel und Constitutionen deren Geistlichen der Congregation Unser
    Frauen von dem Ehrwürdigen Diener Gottes Petro Forerrio.
    Eichstätt: 1721.
Regula et Constitutiones Clericorum regularium ministrantium
    infirmis. Rome: 1727.
Regula et Constitutiones Fratrum Poenitentium Tertii Ordinis Sc.
    Francisi Congregationis Gallicanae Strictae Observantiae. Paris:
    1773.
Regula Primitiva et Constitutiones Fratrum Discalceatorum
    Congregationis Hispaniae Ordinis Sanctissimae Trinitatis
    Redemptionis Captivorum. Madrid: 1787.

Bibliography

Regula S. P. Benedicti et Constitutiones Congregationis S. Mauri. Paris: 1770.

Regula S. P. Benedicti et Constitutiones Congregationis SS. Vitoni et Hydulphi. Paris: 1774.

Reiffenstuel, Anaclet. *Jus canonicum universum: clara methodo iuxta titulos quinqve librorum decretalium in quæstiones distributum, solidisque responsionibus, & objectionum solutionibus dilucidatum [1714].* Vol. 5. Venice: 1735.

Romanus, Franz Wilhelm, and Wilhelm Ludwig Brummer. *Dissertatio juridica . . . de perrara poena ad triremes in illis constitutionibus.* Leipzig: 1730.

Sambuca, Michael. *Constitutiones et statuta generalia cismontanae familiae Ordinis Sancti Francisci de Observantia ex decretis Capituli Generalis Romani anni 1639 & Toletani Anni 1658 compilata.* Venice: 1718.

Sanchez, Thomas. *Consilia seu Opuscula Moralia: Opus Posthumum. Editio Ultima a Mendis Expurgata.* Vol. 2. Lyon: 1681.

Schickard, Wilhelm. *Jus Regium Hebræorum e tenebris Rabbinicis erutum et luci donatum.* Argentinae: 1625.

Sgroi, Didacus. *Lux praelatorum, praesertim regularium, necnon etiam curiae saecularis foro criminali tum theorice, tum practica accensa.* Venice: 1673.

Simon, Jordan. *Institutiones Canonicae sive corollaria ex universo jure historico ecclesiastico.* Erfurt: 1770.

Sinistrari, Ludovicus. *De delictis, et poenis tractatus absolutissimus.* Rome: 1754.

————. *Formularium Criminale.* Rome: 1754.

————. *Practica Criminalis Illustrata hoc est commentarii perpetui, et absolute in practicam criminalem Fratrum Minorum.* 2 vols. Rome: 1693.

Sonnenfels, Joseph von. *Grundsätze der Polizey, Handlung und Finanzwissenschaft.* Vol. 1. 3rd ed. Vienna: 1770.

Spenn, Joseph. *Lebensbeschreibung Joseph Spenns, ehemaligen Katholiken und Augustinermönchs.* Magdeburg: 1805.

Statuta Generalia Cismontanae Familiae Ordinis Fratrum Minorum Sancti Francisci Reformatorum in capitulo generali Anno 1639. Prague: 1677.

Statuta Provincialia Fratrum Minorum Recollectorum Provinciae Comitatus Flandriae S. Josephi [1718]. Brugge: 1719.

Stromberg, Christian von. *Denkwürdiger und nützlicher Antiquarius . . . Mittelrhein.* Vol. II/1. Coblenz: 1851.

Weber, Karl Julius. *Die Möncherey.* 4 vols. Stuttgart: 1818–20.

SECONDARY SOURCES

Aigner, Thomas. "Überlegungen zu Herkunft, Leben und sozialer Vernetzung der Aggsbacher Kartäuser." In *Die Reichskartause Buxheim 1402–2002*, edited by James Hogg et al., 2:13–30. Salzburg: Analecta Cartusiana, 2004.

Alfieri, Fernanda. *Nella camera degli sposi: Tomás Sánchez, il matrimonio, la sessualità (secoli XVI–XVII)*. Bologna: Soc. Ed. Il Mulino, 2010.

Ammerer, Gerhard, ed. *Orte der Verwahrung die innere Organisation von Gefängnissen, Hospitälern und Klöstern seit dem Spätmittelalter*. Leipzig: Leipziger Univ.-Verlag, 2010.

Bamford, Paul. *Fighting Ships and Prisons: The Mediterranean Galleys of France in the Age of Louis XIV*. Minneapolis: University of Minnesota Press, 1973.

Beales, Derek. *Joseph II: Against the World*. Cambridge: Cambridge University Press, 2010.

———. *Prosperity and Plunder: European Catholic Monasteries in the Age of Revolution, 1650–1815*. Cambridge: Cambridge University Press, 2003.

Beattie, J. M. "Scales of Justice: Defense Counsel and the English Criminal Trial in the Eighteenth and Nineteenth Centuries." *Law and History Review* 9 (1991) 221–67.

Bedouelle, Guy. *The Reform of Catholicism, 1480–1620*. Translated by James K. Farge. Toronto: Pontifical Institute of Mediaeval Studies, 2008.

Binhack, Franz. "Drei Jahre aus der Geschichte der Abtei Waldsassen, 1792–1795." *Cistercienser-Chronik* 12 (1900) 257–64.

———. "Geschichte des Cistercienser-Stiftes Waldsassen in den Jahren 1798 und 1799 (II)." *Cistercienser-Chronik* 11 (1899) 266–70.

Boguth, Walter. "Die Aufhebung der Kartause Mauerbach." *Jahrbuch für Landeskunde von Niederösterreich* 1 (1902) 297–312.

Cassidy-Welch, Megan. *Imprisonment in the Medieval Religious Imagination, c.1150–1400*. Houndmills, UK: Palgrave Macmillan, 2011.

———. "Incarceration and Liberation: Prisons in the Cistercian Monasteries." *Viator* 32 (2001) 23–42.

Castan, Nicole, and André Zysberg, eds. *Histoire des galères, bagnes et prisons de France de l'Ancien Régime*. Toulouse: Privat, 2002.

Bibliography

Cattaneo, Mario. *Aufklärung und Strafrecht. Beiträge zur deutschen Strafrechtsphilosophie des 18. Jahrhunderts*. Berlin: Nomos, 1998.

Chadwick, Owen. *The Popes and European Revolution*. Oxford: Oxford University Press, 1981.

Châtellier, Louis. *The Europe of the Devout: The Catholic Reformation and the Formation of a New Society*. Cambridge: Cambridge University Press, 1989.

———. *The Religion of the Poor: Rural Missions in Europe and the Formation of Modern Catholicism, c.1500–c.1880*. Translated by Brian Pearce. Cambridge: Cambridge University Press, 1993.

Chevallier, Pierre. *Lomenie de Brienne et l'ordre monastique, 1766–1789*. Vol. 1. Paris: Librairie philosophique J. Vrin, 1958.

Clark, Anthony E. *China's Saints: Catholic Martyrdom during the Qing, 1644–1911*. Bethlehem, PA: Lehigh University Press, 2011.

Connery, John R. *Abortion: The Development of the Roman Catholic Perspective*. Chicago: Loyola University Press, 1977.

Danz, Wilhelm August F. *Grundsätze der summarischen Prozesse*. Edited by Nikolaus T. Gönner. 3rd ed. Stuttgart: 1806.

Decker, Rainer. *Witchcraft and the Papacy: An Account Drawing on the Formerly Secret Records of the Roman Inquisition*. Translated by Erik Midelfort. Charlottesville: University of Virginia Press, 2008.

Dülmen, Richard van. *Theater des Schreckens. Gerichtspraxis und Strafrituale in der frühen Neuzeit*. 4th ed. Munich: C.H. Beck, 1995. In English: *Theater of Terror*. Cambridge: Blackwell, 1990.

Egan, Keith. "John of the Cross." In *Biographical Dictionary of Christian Theologians*, edited by Patrick W. Carey, 282–83. Westport, CT: Greenwood, 2000.

Evans, Robert. *The Fabrication of Virtue: English Prison Architecture, 1750–1840*. Cambridge: Cambridge University Press, 1982.

Finzsch, Norbert, and Robert Jütte, eds. *Institutions of Confinement: Hospitals, Asylums, and Prisons in Western Europe and North America, 1500–1950*. Cambridge: Cambridge University Press, 1996.

Fossier, Arnaud. "La pénitencerie pontificale en Avignon (XIVe s.) ou la justice des âmes comme style de gouvernement." In *Les justices d'Église dans le Midi (XIe-XVe siècle)*, 199–239. Toulouse: Privat, 2007.

———. "Propter vitandum scandalum. Histoire d'une catégorie juridique (XIIe-XVe siècles)." *Mélanges de l'Ecole française de Rome, Moyen Âge* 121 (2009) 317–48.

Foucault, Michel. *Histoire de la sexualité*. Paris: Gallimard, 1976.

———. *Madness and Civilization. A History of Insanity in the Age of Reason* [*Folie et déraison, 1961*]. London: Routledge, 2001.

———. *Überwachen und Strafen. Die Geburt des Gefängnisses* [*Surveiller et punir*]. Frankfurt: Suhrkamp, 1976.

Frauenstädt, P. "Zur Galeerenstrafe in Deutschland." *Zeitschrift für die gesamte Strafrechtswissenschaft* 16 (1896) 518–46.

Garner, Bryan, ed. *Black's Law Dictionary*. 7th ed. St. Paul, MN: West Group, 1999.

Geltner, Guy. *The Medieval Prison: A Social History*. Princeton: Princeton University Press, 2008.

Gray, Robert. *Lineations*. Todmorden: Arc, 1998.

Grell, Ole Peter, Andrew Cunningham, and Bernd Roeck, eds. *Health Care and Poor Relief in 18th and 19th Century Southern Europe*. Aldershot: Ashgate, 2005.

Hartmann, Wilfried. *Kirche und Kirchenrecht um 900: Die Bedeutung der spätkarolingischen Zeit für Tradition und Innovation im kirchlichen Recht*. Hannover: Hahnsche Buchhandlung, 2008.

Hemmerle, Josef. *Die Benediktinerabtei Benediktbeuern*. Germania Sacra NF 28. Berlin: de Gruyter, 1991.

Heufelder, Emmanuel Maria. "Strenge und Milde. Die Strafkapitel der Benediktinerregel." *Benediktinische Monatsschrift* 28 (1952) 6–18.

Heullant-Donat, Isabelle, et al., eds. *Enfermements: le cloître et la prison, VIe-XVIIIe siècle*. Paris: Publications de la Sorbonne, 2011.

Hofmeister, Philipp. "Vom Strafverfahren bei den Ordensleuten." *Archiv für katholisches Kirchenrecht* 124 (1950) 24–78.

Hull, Isabell. *Sexuality, State and Civil Society, 1700–1815*. Ithaca: Cornell University Press, 1996.

Hurel, Daniel-Odon. "La prison et la charité. Les enjeux contradictoires de l'enfermement pour faute grave dans l'Ordre de Saint-Benoît à l'époque moderne." In *Enfermements: le cloître et la prison, VIe-XVIIIe siècle*, edited by Isabelle Heullant-Donat et al., 119–33. Paris: Publications de la Sorbonne, 2011.

Jäger, Hans-Wolf. "Mönchskritik und Klostersatire in der deutschen Spätaufklärung." In *Katholische Aufklärung—Aufklärung im katholischen Deutschland*, edited by Harm Klueting, 192–207. Hamburg: Meiner, 1993.

Jerouschek, Günther. "Die Herausbildung des peinlichen Inquisitionsprozesses im Spätmittelalter und in der frühen

Bibliography

Neuzeit." *Zeitschrift für die gesamte Strafrechtswissenschaft* 104 (1992) 328–60.

———. "Jenseits von Gut und Böse. Das Geständnis und seine Bedeutung im Strafrecht." *Zeitschrift für die gesamte Strafrechtswissenschaft* 102 (1990) 793–819.

Jütte, Robert. "Syphilis and Confinement: Hospitals in Early Modern Germany." In *Institutions of Confinement*, edited by Norbert Finzsch and Robert Jütte, 97–115. Cambridge: Cambridge University Press, 1996.

Kéry, Lotte. *Gottesfurcht und irdische Strafe: Der Beitrag des mittelalterlichen Kirchenrechts zur Entstehung des öffentlichen Strafrechts*. Cologne: Böhlau, 2006.

Kober, Franz Quirin von. "Die Gefängnissstrafe gegen Cleriker und Mönche." *Theologische Quartalschrift* 59 (1877) 3–74; 551–635.

———. "Die körperliche Züchtigung als kirchliches Strafmittel gegen Kleriker und Mönche." *Theologische Quartalschrift* 57 (1875) 3–78.

Koch, Arnd. *Denunciatio: Zur Geschichte eines strafprozessualen Rechtsinstituts*. Frankfurt: Klostermann, 2006.

Krauss, Karl F. A. *Im Kerker vor und nach Christus: Schatten und Licht aus dem profanen und kirchlichen Cultur- und Rechtsleben vergangener Zeiten*. Freiburg i.B.: Mohr, 1895.

Kwiatkowski, Ernst von. *Die Constitutio Criminalis Theresiana*. Innsbruck: Wagner, 1904.

Landau, Peter. "Das Weihehindernis der Illegitimität in der Geschichte." In *Illegitimität im Spätmittelalter*, edited by Ludwig Schmugge, 41–53. Munich: Oldenbourg, 1994.

Langbein, John H. *Prosecuting Crime in the Renaissance: England, Germany, France*. Cambridge: Harvard University Press, 1974.

———. "The Prosecutorial Origins of Defence Counsel in the Eighteenth Century: The Appearance of Solicitors." *Cambridge Law Journal* 58 (1999) 314–65.

———. *Torture and the Law of Proof: Europe and England in the Ancien Régime*. Chicago: University of Chicago Press, 1977.

Leclerq, Jean. *Libérez les prisonniers: Du bon larron à Jean XXIII*. Paris: Cerf, 1976.

Lehner, Ulrich L. *Enlightened Monks: The German Benedictines 1740–1803*. Oxford: Oxford University Press, 2011.

Lesaulnier, Jean. *Port-Royal et la prison*. Paris: Nolin, 2011.

Logan, Donald. *Runaway Religious in Medieval England, c. 1240–1540*. Cambridge: Cambridge University Press, 1996.

Lusset, Élisabeth. "Entre les murs. L'enfermement punitif des religieux criminels au sein du cloître (XII-XV s.)." In *Enfermements: Le cloître et la prison, VI-XVIII siècle,* edited by Isabelle Heullant-Donat et al., 153–68. Paris: Publications de la Sorbonne, 2011.

———. "Propriae salutis immemores? Réflexions sur la correction des moniales criminelles en Occident, XIIIe-XVe s." In *Figures de femmes criminelles: De l'Antiquité à nos jours,* edited by L. Cadiet et al., 255–65. Paris: Publications de la Sorbonne, 2010.

Maasburg, Friedrich von. *Die Galeerenstrafe in den deutschen und böhmischen Erbländern Oesterreichs.* Vienna: 1885.

Maass, Ferdinand, ed. *Der Josephinismus: Quellen zu seiner Geschichte in Österreich 1760–1850.* Vol. 3. Vienna: Herold, 1956.

Mangei, Johannes. "Klosterhaft und Klosterregel—Aussenseiter in monastischen Gemeinschaften." In *Exil, Fremdheit und Ausgrenzung in Mittelalter und früher Neuzeit,* edited by Andreas Bihrer, 61–71. Würzburg: Ergon, 2000.

Marmursztejn, Elsa. "Issues obligatoires: Clôture et incarcération dans la pensée scolastique des XIIIe-XIVe siècles." In *Enfermements: le cloître et la prison, VIe-XVIIIe siècle,* edited by Isabelle Heullant-Donat et al., 71–88. Paris: Publications de la Sorbonne, 2011

May, Georg. *Das Priesterhaus in Marienborn.* Mainz: Bistum Mainz, 2005.

McManners, John. *Church and Society in Eighteenth-Century France.* 2 vols. Oxford: Oxford University Press, 1999.

Meyer, Frédéric. "Religiosi fuorillegge: i Regolari di fronte alla Giustizia in Savoia nel secolo XVIII." In *Quaderni Storici. Nuova Serie* 119 (2005) 519–53.

Mikoletzky, Lorenz. "Klosterkerker–Korrektionshäuser. Aus den Materialien der Geistlichen Hofkommission und der Vereinigten Hofkanzlei." In *Ecclesia Peregrinans. Josef Lenzenweger zum 70. Geburtstag,* edited by Karl Amon, 257–63. Vienna: Verband der Wissenschaftlichen Gesellschaften Österreichs, 1986.

Muchembled, Robert. *L'Invention de l'homme moderne: sensibilités, moeurs et comportements collectifs sous l'Ancien régime.* Paris: Fayard, 1988.

Müller, Daniela. "Der Einfluss der Kirche." In *Die Durchsetzung des öffentlichen Strafanspruchs: Systematisierung der Fragestellung,* edited by Klaus Lüderssen, 69–94. Cologne: Böhlau, 2002.

Bibliography

O'Leary, Charles Gerard. *Religious Dismissed after Perpetual Profession: An Historical Conspectus and Commentary*. Catholic University of America Canon Law Studies 184. Washington, DC: Catholic University of America Press, 1943.

Petz, Wolfgang. *Die letzte Hexe: Das Schicksal der Anna Maria Schwäglin*. Frankfurt: Campus, 2007.

Plath, Christian. "Ein Beispiel klösterlicher Jurisdiktion im 18. Jahrhundert: Der Fall des Franziskanerpaters Wendelin Heun." *Zeitschrift für die Geschichte des Oberrheins* 154 (2006) 271–82.

Porter, Roy. *Madness: A History.* Oxford: Oxford University Press, 2002.

Puff, Helmut. "Early Modern Europe, 1400–1700." In *Gay Life and Culture: A World History*, edited by Robert Aldrich, 78–101. New York: Universe, 2006.

———. *Sodomy in Reformation Germany and Switzerland, 1400–1600*. Chicago: University of Chicago Press, 2003.

Pugh, Ralph. *Imprisonment in Medieval England*. Cambridge: Cambridge University Press, 1968.

Rapley, Elizabeth. *A Social History of the Cloister: Daily Life in the Teaching Monasteries of the Old Regime*. Montreal: McGill-Queen's University Press, 2001.

Renner, Michael. "Jugend- und Studienzeit der Brüder Adam Friedrich und Josef Franz von Seinsheim." *Würzburger Diözesangeschichtsblätter* 49 (1987) 185–300.

Riesner, Albert Joseph. *Apostates and Fugitives from Religious Institutes: An Historical Conspectus and Commentary*. Catholic University of America Canon Law Studies 168. Washington, DC: Catholic University of America Press, 1942.

Ruff, Julius R. *Violence in Early Modern Europe*. Cambridge: Cambridge University Press, 2001.

Rother, Wolfgang. "Zwischen Utilitarismus und Kontraktualismus. Beccarias Kritik an der Todesstrafe im philosophischen Kontext." In *Gegen Folter und Todesstrafe: aufklärerischer Diskurs und europäische Literatur vom 18. Jahrhundert bis zur Gegenwart*, edited by Helmut C. Jacobs, 185–202. Frankfurt: P. Lang, 2007.

Rothschild, Emma. *The Inner Life of Empires: An Eighteenth-Century History*. Princeton: Princeton University Press, 2011.

Rüthing, Heinrich. "Die Wächter Israels: Ein Beitrag zur Geschichte der Visitationen im Kartäuserorden." In *Die Kartäuser: Der Orden der schweigenden Mönche*, edited by Marijan Zadnikar, 169–83. Cologne: Wienand, 1983.

Bibliography

Scherhak, Elisabeth. "Die Klosterkerker in der österreichischen Monarchie des 18. Jahrhunderts: Studien zu ihrer Situation nach staatlichen und kirchlichen Visitationsberichten." PhD thesis, University of Vienna, 1986.

Scholz, Franz. "Die Kartause Mauerbach." *Berichte und Mittheilungen des Alterthums-Vereins zu Wien* 35 (1900) 76–105.

Schreiner, Klaus. "Defectus natalium: Geburt aus einem unrechtmässigen Schoss als Problem klösterlicher Gemeinschaftsbildung." In *Illegitimität im Spätmittelalter*, edited by Ludwig Schmugge et al., 85–114. Munich: Oldenbourg, 1994.

Schmidt, Christine D. *Sühne oder Sanktion? Die öffentliche Kirchenbusse in den Fürstbistümern Münster und Osnabrück während des 17. und 18. Jahrhunderts.* Münster: Aschendorff, 2009.

Schmoeckel, Mathias. *Humanität und Staatsraison: Die Abschaffung der Folter in Europa und die Entwicklung des gemeinsamen Strafprozess- und Beweisrechts seit dem hohen Mittelalter.* Cologne: Böhlau, 2000.

Schutte, Anne Jacobson. *By Force and Fear: Taking and Breaking Monastic Vows in Early Modern Europe.* Ithaca: Cornell University Press, 2011.

Sedatis, L. "Summarischer Prozess." In *Handwörterbuch der Rechtsgeschichte*, edited by Adalbert Erler and Ekkehard Kaufmann, 5:78–80. Berlin: Schmidt, 1998.

Sellin, Thorsten. "Jean Mabillon: A Prison Reformer of the Seventeenth Century." *Journal of the American Institute of Criminal Law and Criminology* 17 (1927) 581–607.

Shubin, Daniel H. *Monastery Prisons: The History of Monasteries as Prisons.* N.p.: D. Shubin, 2001.

Simmert, Johannes. *Die Geschichte der Kartause zu Mainz: Beitrage zur Geschichte der Stadt Mainz 16.* Mainz: 1958.

Spector, Scott, Helmut Puff, and Dagmar Herzog, eds. *After the History of Sexuality: German Genealogies with and Beyond Foucault.* New York: Berghahn, 2012.

Spierenburg, Pieter. "Four Centuries of Prison History: Punishment, Suffering, the Body, and Power." In *Institutions of Confinement: Hospitals, Asylums, and Prisons in Western Europe and North America, 1500–1950*, edited by Norbert Finzsch and Robert Jütte, 17–37. Cambridge: Cambridge University Press, 1996.

Bibliography

————. "From Amsterdam to Auburn: An Explanation for the Rise of the Prison in Seventeenth-Century Holland and Nineteenth-Century America." *Journal of Social History* 20 (1987) 439–61.

————. *The Prison Experience: Disciplinary Institutions in Early Modern Europe.* Amsterdam: Amsterdam University Press, 2007.

Spilker, Reginhard. "Die Busspraxis in der Regel des hl. Benedikt." *Studien und Mitteilungen zur Geschichte des Benediktinerordens* 57 (1939) 12–38.

Ströbele, Ute. *Zwischen Kloster und Welt: Die Aufhebung südwestdeutscher Frauenklöster unter Kaiser Joseph II.* Cologne: Böhlau, 2005.

Stöhlker, Friedrich. "Die Kartause St. Veith in Prüll im Rahmen der Niederdeutschen Provinz des Kartäuserordens." *Die Kartäuser und das Heilige Römische Reich: Internationaler Kongress vom 9.-11. September 1997,* edited by James Hogg, 1:8–65. Salzburg: Institut für Anglistik und Amerikanistik, 1998.

Struber, Rupert. *Priesterkorrektionsanstalten in der Erzdiözese Salzburg im 18. und 19. Jahrhundert: Die Priesterhäuser von Maria Kirchenthal, St. Johann in Tirol, St. Ulrich am Pillersee und Schernberg.* Frankfurt: P. Lang, 2004.

Taeger, Angela. *Intime Machtverhältnisse: Moralstrafrecht und administrative Kontrolle der Sexualität im ausgehenden Ancien Regime.* Munich: Oldenbourg, 1999.

Treiber, Hubert, and Heinz Steinert. *Die Fabrikation des zuverlässigen Menschen: über die "Wahlverwandtschaft" von Kloster- und Fabrikdisziplin.* 2nd. ed. Münster: Westfälisches Dampfboot, 1980; 2005.

Trusen, Winfried. "Der Inquisitionsprozess. Seine historischen Grundlagen und frühen Formen." *Zeitschrift der Savigny-Stiftung für Rechtsgeschichte. Kanonistische Abteilung* 74 (1988) 168–230.

Vanja, Christine. "Madhouses, Children's Wards, and Clinics: The Development of Insane Asylums in Germany." In *Institutions of Confinement: Hospitals, Asylums, and Prisons in Western Europe and North America, 1500–1950,* edited by Norbert Finzsch and Robert Jütte, 117–32. Cambridge: Cambridge University Press, 1996.

Vannotti, Barbara. "Monasterium exivit, et ad seculum est reversa . . . : die Flucht der Schenkin von Erbach aus der Fraumünsterabtei in Zürich." In *Strenarum Lanx. Beiträge zur Philologie des Mittelalters und der Frühen Neuzeit: Festschrift Peter Stotz,* edited by Martin H. Graf and Christian Moser, 187–207. Zurich: Achius, 2003.

———. "Von der entlaufenen Nonne zur Schlossherrin: Magdalena Payer von Hagenwil: Zum Schicksal von Apostatinnen im Spätmittelalter." *Schriften des Vereins für die Geschichte des Bodensees und seiner Umgebung* 124 (2006) 93–110.

Vigorelli, Giancarlo, et al., eds. *Vita e processo di suor Virginia Maria de Leyva, monaca di Monza.* Milan: Garzanti, 1985.

Walter, Rudolf. "Benedikt Geisler: Ein fränkischer Klosterkomponist des 18. Jahrhunderts." *Mainfränkisches Jahrbuch* 42 (1990) 168–93.

Wendehorst, Alfred. *Die Benediktinerabtei und das adelige Säkularkanonikerstift St. Burkard in Würzburg.* Germania Sacra NF 40. Berlin: de Gruyter, 2001.

Wiedemann, Theodor. "Die Klosterkerker in der Erzdiözese Wien." *Österreichische Vierteljahresschrift für katholische Theologie* 10 (1871) 413–42.